The HEALING TOUCH

The

HEALING TOUCH

Experiencing God's Love in the

Midst of Our Pain

TODD OUTCALT

Health Communications, Inc.
Deerfield Beach, Florida

www.hci-online.com

CONTENTS

ACKNOWLEDGMENTS

*T*he writing of a book—and certainly *this particular* book—owes its birth and existence to many people.

I am particularly indebted to my family—Becky, Chelsey and Logan—for providing space and time for me to share my thoughts with others. To Becky, a special thanks for allowing me to tell our story and the continued healing we experience each day.

Thanks also to the people who opened their lives to me or allowed me to interview them for this book. Not all of you are mentioned here by name—some names and circumstances have been changed to protect privacy—but I am grateful for your witness to God's touch and for allowing me to tell your stories.

There were others who faithfully read early drafts of the manuscript and offered insight and support. Toward this end, I am grateful to Alda and Jack Andrews—and especially Alda's keen awareness of God's healing, despite so many physical setbacks. Bob and Luela McBride—thank you—especially Dr. McBride, for your keen theological notes. Ray and Nancy Alexander—my thanks for reading so thoroughly and catching my mistakes. Bill and Beverly Riffle—you have my gratitude. And to Beverly, what a wonder of healing you are to so many others; I enjoy your stories, your theological shrewdness and the sticky notes. And to Jerry Steadham, who always seems to offer healing when I need it most—thanks for the talks, for the affirming word and for allowing me to use your perfect subtitles in each of the chapters. In my book, you are the real Dr. Incredible!

I must also express gratitude to the congregations I have served—and to the people who have been a part of this book in both support and affirmation.

Looking back, I can also see that the book itself would never have been conceived had it not been for a sabbatical grant provided by the Lilly Foundation. The experience of renewal was a high point in my ministry and several of the chapters were made possible through the writing space and retreat this leave offered.

Portions of this book were also previously published (in slightly different form) in *Cure* and *Together* magazines. I appreciate Kathy LaTour and Melissa Weber for providing so many helpful articles, and a fine magazine on the healing arts, and also Dan Gangler, for giving me the opportunity to write about these matters through a monthly column.

By the time any person holds this book in hand, it goes without saying that the pages themselves spring to life only because of a committed publisher. Toward that end, I am grateful to everyone at Health Communications, Inc. Peter Vegso—thanks for giving me this opportunity! Thank you also, Susan Heim, for believing in this book, serving as editor and offering so much of yourself to this project.

Finally, I owe much to the readers, for whom I write. You have my gratitude. Also, thanks to Amy Hughes for serving as editor, renewing the project, and making the most of my manuscript. May this be the first of many books together, Amy!

INTRODUCTION

What Does It Mean to Be "Healed"?

$\mathcal{M}$ost commonly, when people hear the word "healing," they are struck with images that may lie far outside of the purview of their own experiences: scenes from a Hollywood movie where someone miraculously rises from the bed and walks; images of a faith healer "laying hands" upon an adoring entourage of sick people who have arrived onstage in wheelchairs and on crutches; or, perhaps, a new medication, a new surgical procedure or a cutting-edge discovery that will eliminate a disease or malady forever. These images stick with us, despite our lack of personal experience with healing.

Likewise, most people picture some type of physical renewal when they hear the word "healing." A person is sick; he miraculously becomes well. Another person is told she will live only two months because of a heart disease—but lives ten years in a state of restored health. Another is diagnosed with a cancerous tumor—but the disease evaporates overnight.

Of course, such miraculous or seemingly unexplainable events do occur, and we could all probably tell our own stories of the people we have known and the miracles that have been wrought in our circles of friendship and family.

But there is more to healing—at least the healing that is portrayed in the scriptures—beyond the absence of disease. After all, not everyone who has faith in God recovers from illness. Not all terminally ill patients rise from their beds and walk. Not all tumors evaporate. In fact, most people with serious illnesses do not recover. This is a fact of life. And this truth is clearly portrayed in the scriptures—for the Bible tells us that death comes to all, and that God desires to help us in our infirmities and weaknesses (though we are not *promised* deliverance from illness and death).

Does this mean, however, that God does not heal?

Quite the contrary. God can and does heal people. But our concepts of healing need to be broadened considerably if we are to glimpse more fully the complete work of God.

Consider—as we continue on the theme of the physical, the body—how often our concept of "healing" can be substituted with the word "cure." In actuality, "cure" is what we are talking about when we discuss the notion of someone being healed of a disease. *This person was cured of his tumor,* we might say. Or, *I know a woman who was given only two months to live, but she was cured.*

In all honesty, "cure" is what we desire when we are ill. We are sick—we want to be well. We have the flu—we want relief. Our back aches—we long to be pain free.

This is "cure."

But healing may be something else entirely. A cure has to do with physical well-being. But healing may reach far beyond the physical and touch us in other ways—perhaps not in a physical manner at all. Likewise, a person who has not been cured of a disease may still receive God's healing. And there are other times when our true healing may not be attached to anything physical at all—but may have more to do with our minds, our emotions or our relationships with other people. Stress can make us ill just as easily as a flu bug. Depression can break down our bodies and weaken our immune systems. A broken marriage, a wayward child or a family situation can cause us as much heartache—or more—than an actual heart attack.

So when we speak of cure, we are actually talking about being restored to a pre-illness condition. Healing, on the other hand, is a new fullness of life that may reach far beyond the cure.

Perhaps a couple of personal stories might help to illustrate these truths.

Some years ago, I received a phone call on a Saturday morning from a nurse in a mental health facility. The staff at this hospital was looking for a pastor to come and hear the "confession" of a young man who had admitted himself into their drug rehab program. I agreed to go, not knowing what I would find, or what, specifically, I would be asked to do.

Soon after arriving, I was ushered into a small back room where I sat in a chair facing a young man—a patient no more than twenty-five years old—who looked as though he were carrying the weight of the world on his shoulders. I was told that this fellow needed to talk to someone—someone who could offer him God's forgiveness—and that it was my role to hear his confession and offer him absolution for his sins.

Not being a priest, this was new territory for me, and I was nervous. But I did listen. In fact, I listened for more than two hours as this young man laid out the details of his life: scenes of a father who had abused him, his life of promiscuity and drug addiction, his thefts, his lies, his adultery and much more. At times, as this man talked, he would pace the floor, pound on the walls, beat his chest or scream. But the longer he talked and the more he confessed, the calmer he became.

There was no doubt that this young man had reached the "end of his rope." He wanted God's help. And he was longing to be healed.

But the healing he was seeking had nothing to do with the physical—although his body had certainly been abused and worn by the stresses of his life.

As our session wound to a close, I was reminded of words found in the book of James (5:16): "Confess your sins to one another, and pray for one another, that you may be healed." And I also was reminded of the many times when Jesus said, "Your sins are forgiven" as a prelude to healing.

There are connections between forgiveness and healing, and certainly there was an obvious connection between this young man's healing and his confession. As he knelt on the floor and I placed my hands upon his head and said a prayer on his behalf, I could literally feel the tension releasing from his body. He gave a great sigh of relief, as all of the sins and destructive patterns of his life were offered up to God. His muscles relaxed, his hands ceased to shake in anger and sorrow and his tears were both freeing and cleansing.

I have to say that I witnessed a healing that day—although there was very little of the "physical" about it. Rather, it was an emotional and spiritual event.

Since that time, I've witnessed many instances where confession of sin or recognition of need brings healing to an individual. I've seen how the ability to open ourselves to others, and to God, often brings spiritual or relational renewal. And I've seen how people have struggled through serious illnesses—some surviving, others dying—only to give testimony to healing far beyond the physical.

Healing comes in many forms.

Witness another example.

A few years back, I recall receiving an unexpected visitor at the church office one summer afternoon. An older woman from the congregation had dropped by to talk. I knew her well. I had officiated at the funeral for her husband some months before. I knew her children (all grown and living out of the house) and her grandchildren. I knew most of her friends. But since she had come to see me, I assumed she had a problem to discuss, a mystery for me to solve.

However, as she talked, she offered no questions, no hints that might inform me of her difficulties or problems. I tried to listen, but found myself offering leading questions of my own, apparent attempts to get to the root of her need. But these attempts failed. Eventually I just sat and listened. And then I realized. She was not seeking my opinion or help at all—but my friendship. It was obvious that she had dropped by to see me because she was lonely. She simply wanted someone to talk to.

As we closed our time together, she asked me to pray for her—which I did—and once again, I could see a change in her physical expression. It was a healing in a small way—but important to her—this relational restoration, the opportunity to talk to someone who was willing to be a part of her life.

Of course, this is such a simple observation, yet a reality for many people in our world today. So many people are afraid; they feel isolated and alone; they are frightened, not by the threat of disease or death, but by the sound of their own breathing, the constant reminders that they have lost something or someone. If only there was someone to talk to, to share life with, to sit beside through the long hours of the day. There is a need of such healing in our world today—and it staggers the imagination.

Reflecting on this dear woman's experience, I wonder: was her restoration any less of a healing than that experienced by someone cured of cancer? Was God's intervention any less real to her than to one who receives a triple bypass? Wasn't her heart stirred and lifted by a human touch, by another voice?

There can be no doubt that relationships are instrumental in our healing. When we look at the healing accounts recorded in the Bible—particularly the healing stories of Jesus—it is worth noting that all of them have a strong relational or social component to them.

How many relational and social healings might be needed in our world today? Isolation, loneliness and fear seem to dominate the landscape of our lives—especially in America where individualism and upward mobility eat away at our sense of connection and care. There is a deep need for people to rediscover a sense of community. We all need someone to love us. And we all need someone to love.

More Questions

In his pastoral memoir, *Open Secrets,* Richard Lischer tells the story of a teenage girl in his congregation who came to him with questions about divine healing.[1] Lischer, a young Lutheran pastor at the time, had mixed feelings about this girl's decision to attend a "healing service" conducted by a well-known evangelist in a huge sports arena. *What,* he wondered, *did this say about the effectiveness of his own ministry? Could God really heal this girl and allow her to rise from her wheelchair? If she wasn't healed, what would this do to her faith? And even if she could not walk again, might God provide some other form of healing or grace?*

Like Richard Lischer, most Christians have questions about God's healing. What is it? Does healing really happen? Why don't "miracles" happen in church? Or do they? Should we be so presumptuous as to ask for God's healing when there is so much misery in the world? What might God's healing look like if we were to receive it?

Perhaps you have asked such questions. Perhaps you have wrestled with these matters. I hope so. That is what this book is about. It is an opportunity to explore the ways in which God intervenes and intersects with our lives, our hopes and our world. This book is an opportunity for people to deepen their understanding of God's healing touch and the ways in which God's grace sustains, renews and regenerates our bodies, minds, relationships and spirits.

I hope that others will be blessed through the exploration itself. For sometimes in the journey, we discover the destination.

Ultimately, of course, healing is God's work—either through God's intervention or through the hands, lips, services and words of others. You and I can be a part of this healing work. This is also a part of the good news. It is where we begin—with our own personal experiences.

For whether we realize it or not, we have all been touched by God.

You have been blessed.

So have I.

God has showered us in love. Here is where all healing begins.

A Personal Story

Little did I know that soon after I began writing this book, my family would be touched with God's healing in a mighty way. I had no idea that I would find myself asking for God's healing. But my prayer came at a most unexpected time.

My wife was at a pharmaceutical sales meeting in Orlando, Florida, when she called with the news. "I just talked to the doctor about the breast biopsy," she said, her voice trembling. "It's not good. I have cancer."

The word stunned me. *Cancer.* How could this be? My wife was too young to have cancer. She was too active, too fit, too conscientious to be diagnosed with this disease. *This must be a mistake,* I thought. My wife was healthy; she ate the best foods; she exercised. And besides, she was busy being a mother and wife. She had a promising career in the medical industry. Like me, she didn't have time for this disease.

Cancer didn't seem like a good match for us. My wife and I were, after all, best friends and lovers. We were parents to two wonderful children. And after seventeen years of marriage we were just beginning to hit our stride—paying off a mortgage, saving for our children's educations, attending school functions and athletic events. How could cancer invade our lives so suddenly, so mercilessly?

A thousand miles away my wife began to sob over the phone.

"We'll get through this," I said. "Take it easy."

Take it easy? How? We'd been waiting for the results of the breast biopsy for five days. But neither of us had dreamed that the test would come back positive. We had considered the biopsy just another procedure, another step following on the heels of a suspicious-looking mammogram—a mere precautionary measure. There was nothing to worry about.

My wife had flown to Florida just two days after the September 11 tragedy. She had a job to do. Everyone, from the president on down, had been telling us to live our lives, to go about our business, to travel. There was nothing to fear. In the aftermath of a national tragedy, the breast biopsy loomed as little more than another medical hoop that my wife was being asked to jump through. The doctors had assured us that biopsies came back negative 80 percent of the time. A person playing Russian roulette could live with those odds.

Suddenly, however, we had to deal with the bullet. My wife was no longer in the majority, but the minority—that silent few (one out of nine women in a lifetime) who develop breast cancer.

"What am I going to do?" my wife sobbed. "How am I going to deal with this?"

As a pastor, I'd helped hundreds of families deal with a multitude of illnesses—many of them terminal. I'd stood by the bedside, offered words of comfort, held trembling hands. I'd presided over funerals and tragedies of every kind. I'd seen heart disease, AIDS, car crash victims and yes, even cancer. A few days before, I had been overwhelmed by the shock of September 11 and had stayed busy organizing prayer vigils and worship services for those who were having difficulty managing their own pain and fear. But nothing had prepared me to help my own wife in her hour of need. The news had entered our lives like an earthquake, and I was too close to the epicenter.

"It's going to be all right," I assured my wife over the phone, trying desperately to believe it myself.

"I can't stay here," my wife told me. "I want to come home. I love you. I need to be with you."

"Come home," I said. "I love you, too."

That was that. But the hard part was just beginning.

Later that evening, my wife's flight roared into Indianapolis at midnight—the last flight of the day. When we made eye contact, we walked toward one another slowly, arms outstretched and aching for touch (just like some scene from a sappy

Hollywood love story) and fell into each other's arms. We hugged tightly, my wife's face pressing deeply into my chest as she cried. I looked far off, searching for some sign beyond the windows, hoping that this strange and awkward moment might turn out to be just a bad dream.

I didn't want to cry. I wanted to be strong—for her, for our children, for the future. But inside my chest my heart was pounding and I struggled for some words of faith and encouragement. "It will be all right," I kept mouthing over and over. "Don't worry."

There would be new worries, of course.

Over the next few days a plethora of books and pamphlets invaded my life. I read more about breast cancer than I ever wanted to know. Suddenly, everywhere I turned it seemed, there was some new study about mammograms in the newspaper, another television special about breast cancer, an interview with a cancer survivor. When I shared the news with my congregation, an astounding number of women stepped forward to offer my wife their words of comfort and empathy. Dozens of these women were breast cancer survivors themselves. I had no idea.

That first week we received cards and letters by the basketful. People called. Others visited. Many offered their presence to my wife, and to me, in the midst of our storm.

My wife and I began to pray for God's healing—in whatever form we might experience it. We waited, and we wondered— would God heal my wife's body? Would God help us to find the path to wholeness—to a cancer-free world?

A week later, after the initial shock had worn off, my wife set up appointments with a surgeon and a radiologist. We spent the better part of an entire day sweating it out in the sterile confines of a medical center waiting room, surrounded by the faces of others who were weighed down with the same fears and curiosities. There were women who emerged alone from examination rooms—many of them bald or incredibly thin—their faces slack and haggard. Some wore scarves or wigs. Very few seemed to have the support of a man.

Sitting next to my wife, I was overcome by a deepening sadness, not only for our loss and the growing awareness of what we were facing together, but also for the women who were coping with their cancer alone. Where were the husbands, I wondered? The boyfriends? The fathers?

After hours of waiting, we finally spoke to the surgeon—a gentle and articulate doctor who made eye contact with us and reviewed the various options and forms of treatment step-by-step. We talked for an hour, the doctor answering our questions in numbing detail. Later, when we had finished, he sent us down the hallway to speak to a plastic surgeon. More waiting. More discussion. And by the end of the day, we were both wiped out—emotionally, intellectually, physically.

Because of our educational backgrounds, I suppose, and because my wife was a pharmaceutical sales rep, she wanted all the information she could find about breast cancer and treatments. Together we read a startling number of books within a span of days—perhaps more books than I had consumed in any abbreviated period of my life, including graduate school. My wife, particularly, became an expert in the research, philosophy and statistics of breast cancer treatments. She was focused on beating the disease and making the decision that was best for her.

All I could do was watch . . . and lend support. Sometimes I listened. Sometimes I cursed. Sometimes I cried. I prayed, too, of course. I prayed for grace.

Eventually my wife settled into a calmer state of mind—very focused, intense, purposeful. The surgeon had given my wife two options to consider and she was determined to make the right choice. She could have a lumpectomy followed by six weeks of radiation treatments, or opt for a mastectomy followed by reconstructive surgery. These two options weighed on us like giant stones, and my wife feared that her life might be hanging in the balance. Two choices. But which one was best for her?

Being the man didn't help matters, either. I was equally ambivalent. Confused. There were times when I thought to myself, *There must be another choice.* Surely we would awaken to another solution that everyone had overlooked initially—a solution that would not require such drastic measures.

Some evenings, as we sat on the couch in silence, a pile of books between us, my wife would ask the simple and direct question. "I should get a mastectomy, don't you think?"

"Yes," I'd answer. "If that's what you want."

"But what do *you* think?"

"I think you should do what you think is best."

"But . . ."

As time went by, it was clear that, even though I had the best of intentions and my support was unwavering, my wife felt very alone. After all, she was the one who had cancer, not me. She was the one who was going to endure the pain and discomfort of surgery or therapy. It would have to be her decision in the end. All I could do was offer my love and strength.

Later, the surgeon confirmed my suspicions about the isolation and loneliness women face when dealing with breast cancer. When my wife asked the surgeon to recommend an option, he merely shrugged and answered, "You'll have to make that choice." He quickly added, "Some women, like you, immerse themselves in learning about the options. They do their homework; they learn all the medical language and the statistics and the procedures. They know what will be required at every step along the way and they make an informed decision. Other women, however, can't cope with these facts. They feel overwhelmed by knowledge. They just want to get well. They make a decision based on other factors—such as their family situation or how they believe their bodies will react to surgery or treatment. They decide from the heart. In the end, every woman has to make a choice based on what she *knows,* or what she doesn't *want* to know."

Time continued to slip by, and eventually my wife sought a second opinion—not so much because she didn't trust the first surgeon, but because she didn't want to look back later with regret and ask, "Why didn't I pursue other options?" More surgeons, more books, more waiting. Same results. Same options. Same predicament.

Eventually the flow of days pressed for a decision. With breast cancer, time itself has a way of forcing every woman to play her hand. The cards can only be held for so long.

My wife opted for a mastectomy.

Moving into Healing

After this decision was finalized, I learned a great deal about the human psyche, about faith and about God's healing. For example, I learned that any decision we make in life—particularly a weighty one carrying a potential life-and-death outcome— usually bears an accompanying sadness. This reality is all the more pronounced when we are forced to give up some part of the body—particularly an organ associated with our sexuality or identity. To a woman, losing a breast might be akin to a man losing a testicle, or perhaps his libido. The loss of a breast can also cause a woman to relinquish some of her confidence, her hope, even her zest for life. Or just the opposite may be true. Some women will cling all the more to what they need, or may even reprioritize their lives out of a sense of urgency.

Our faith was also stretched in ways we had not experienced before. There was a newfound awareness of the fragility of life— of how utterly dependent we are, each day, upon the unrealized graciousness of God, who gives us life and breath. Every day became a gift to us. Each day offered new opportunities to serve, to love, to draw strength from each other and from friends and family.

And we prayed much for God's healing. A healing that, we believe, my wife eventually received through the intervention of medicine, through prayers, through the life forces that draw us into other people's lives and make us more keenly aware of how God works through science, touch, hope and love.

But during those months of uncertainty, there were many difficulties for my wife. She carried the emotional and psychological weight of losing a breast. And it was difficult for me, too. After all, a man can feel that he is losing something through his wife's surgery—but he may not have the support network or the words to adequately describe this loss.

As I discovered, my wife had access to a wealth of books and pamphlets about breast cancer and how to cope with the disease—but we also had faith, hope and the positive support of so many others to draw from. My wife was surrounded—quickly and caringly—by other women who had gone through the same procedures. And although I initially felt alone and frustrated, other men came to offer me support.

Before the surgery, my wife spent long hours on the telephone discussing all of her options—the solutions and drawbacks—with family and friends. I, on the other hand, spent more time keeping things together at home, helping the children and managing the day-to-day affairs so my wife would have this valuable time to strengthen herself and clear her mind.

These are not complaints, just observations—and I'm sure my wife would agree with them. I was happy to take on this extra load, not only for my wife's sake, but for my own peace of mind and the distractions this busyness afforded me.

As the day of the surgery approached, however, I discovered that I was wrestling with some frightful demons. These fears were largely unspoken, but were real nonetheless. I began to worry about what my wife's breast might look like following the mastectomy—not because I feared that I would be unable or unwilling to look at the scar, but because I feared that my wife might feel unattractive in my presence. I worried that I might not be strong enough to support her and the children through her illness. And, yes, I also worried that, somehow, the sexual chemistry of our marriage or our friendship might be altered.

In one way or another, I dealt with all of these fears . . . and then some. In the end I discovered that, while breast cancer certainly changed my wife, it also changed me. It changed *us*. Not always for the best or for the worst. But the illness did change our outlook on life, our awareness of each other, and it gave us a sharper image of what each of us desired and needed. These observations and realities are also a part of God's healing—the healing that *we experienced*.

I also emerged from this breast cancer ordeal with some firm beliefs about the role men play in the lives of women. There is something instinctive, nearly animalistic, that rises within a man during a time of crisis. There had never been a time in my life when I was so territorial and protective. Although I had never been a soldier, a fireman or a police officer working a beat, I was staking a claim to life, waging a war against an unseen adversary. I protected our evenings, screened phone calls, ran errands. I circled the wagon of our home and marked large Xs on the calendar, blocking off entire days and weeks.

I was able to be the protector when my wife needed strength and reassurance. My nurturing instincts kicked in. I fluffed pillows, cleaned, and prepared breakfast in bed for my wife. I even made French toast and lit candles by the bedside. I performed these tasks without any thought of reward or sexual payback. This was a side of my masculinity I had not explored with much regularity before, and I discovered that I enjoyed making my wife comfortable. In essence, God helped me to change through this ordeal—another sign of grace, a sure presence of healing.

Gradually, our lives began to even out—like syrup expanding over a level plate—and we assumed our familiar way of life. But a part of me remained with my wife's pain—a pain I am reminded of each time I look at her scar.

Now every day counts for something. Together we have made parole; we have beaten the rap; we have been set free to make our way in the world. No matter what obstacles we will face tomorrow—or will ever face at any time in the future—we will be able to size up the problem, and weigh it against what we have received by blessing in the past and the strength and healing that

God has provided through grace. This is the strange outcome of being a cancer survivor, of being the one who walks alongside the patient who has stared death in the face. We are changed. We are healed. We are stronger than we were before.

Introduction Study Guide

The author explores many aspects of healing in the introduction, and also relates several personal stories that may be helpful to the reader. Many of these ideas about healing may be new to people, and yet helpful at the same time. Take a few moments to consider how healing has been evident in your own life and in the lives of those you know. After a brief period of meditation, reflect on or discuss the following questions.

- When you hear the word "healing," what ideas come to mind?
- What were some of the varieties of healing mentioned by the author? Can you think of others?
- Do you know someone who has been healed? How? In what way?
- What connections do you see between forgiveness (or reconciliation with ourselves, others or God) and healing?
- In what ways do the personal stories in the introduction reveal aspects of God's healing?
- What personal testimony could you give (or someone in your family) to God's healing touch?

Close by reading James 5:13–16. What aspects of healing are mentioned in this text? What types of suffering may be alluded to here? How are people involved in healing? In what ways might healing be a cooperative effort between God and people?

Prayer: Gracious God, your healing work is ever present, and yet is also mysterious and elusive to us. Make us mindful of the gifts you have given—talents and abilities that we can use to help and heal each other—as well as a greater awareness of, and faith in, your divine touch. Forgive our sins and heal our diseases, we pray. And help us also to forgive and heal each other. Amen.

CHAPTER 1

Relational Healing:
Changing How We Treat
One Another

*So when you are offering your gift at the altar,
if you remember that your brother or sister has
something against you, leave your gift there before
the altar and go; first be reconciled to your brother
or sister, and then come and offer your gift.*

—Matthew 5:23–24

*M*ost commonly our perceptions of divine healing are intertwined with questions—questions about God's power, about human suffering and the role we must play in our own recovery or the recovery of someone we love. Why is there suffering in the world? If God is good, and all-powerful, then why doesn't God alleviate suffering? Why is there sickness, hunger and death? Where is God when we hurt, and why does God often seem so far away from our problems and difficulties?

We are not the first people to ask such questions, of course. People of faith have struggled with these problems for centuries. In fact, the scriptures are brimming with such theological conundrums. Abraham questioned God's justice. Moses questioned God's purposes and plan. Job longed for God's explanations and argued valiantly with his friends. And many of the Psalms of the Bible address questions pertaining to God's presence, justice or mercy.

Psalm 10 begins with the words: "Why, O Lord, do you stand far off? Why do you hide yourself in times of trouble?"

Psalm 13 begins, "How long, O Lord? Will you forget me forever? How long will you hide your face from me? How long must I bear pain in my soul, and have sorrow in my heart all day long?"

Psalm 22 begins with the words: "My God, my God, why have you forsaken me?" Words that, later, Jesus himself would pray upon the cross, again questioning God's care.

No—we are not the first people to struggle with issues of God's presence and fairness. Like those of old, we too want to know why God doesn't come to our rescue. When we hurt, we want an answer to our suffering, our pain, our loneliness. Often, we wonder why God doesn't heal more of what ails us—in our personal lives, our bodies and in our world. We wonder why people can't get along and why our human relationships are often so fraught with struggle and pain.

THE PAIN OF BEING HUMAN

Certainly, these questions continue to be a part of our faith journey. But one observation rises to the surface when we examine life more closely. We see that there is much suffering in the world, and that there are many forms of this suffering. Yes, there are many forms of physical injury and pain. People are hungry, others thirsty. Some cannot walk. Others cannot speak.

But if we look more deeply, we can also see that not all suffering is of the physical variety. In fact, much of the suffering we experience in life has little to do with the body at all. There are times, for example, when our feelings may be injured. There are times when we feel angry or embarrassed because we did not get accepted into a university or win a coveted prize or competition. Sometimes we have family problems or parenting difficulties or marital stresses. There are misunderstandings, hurtful words, broken friendships. We feel pain when we lose a job, make a mistake or do not receive some reward or accolade that we feel we deserve.

In fact, if we are honest with ourselves, I think we'd agree that most of the pain we experience in life has to do with human relationships. To be human means that we must live in relationship with other people—family, friends, strangers, coworkers, clients, neighbors, teammates, classmates—with people who are like us, and with people who are not at all like us. And the truth is—people cause one another pain.

Sometimes we don't get what we need—emotionally, spiritually or financially—from other people. Sometimes we hurt someone else—and this realization causes us pain, too!

Jesus certainly understood these realities. He knew what it was like to have friends—and to be hurt by his friends. He knew what it was like to have people use him, or abuse him or even ignore him. And a great many of his words address the common difficulties that we all experience in this human adventure.

Once, when Jesus taught a multitude of people (as found in Matthew 5–7), he spoke most eloquently about the battered and broken nature of human relationships—including sorrow, hatred, adultery, love, prayer and murder. At one point, when Jesus was talking about our relationship with God (seeking God's reconciliation), he paused and added, "But suppose you are on your way to worship God, and you remember that something is not right between you and another person. First go and make things right with that person, and then come and make things right with God" (my paraphrase).

Jesus understood that one of the basic human needs is relational healing. We need to be healed of our apathy, our hatred, our prejudice, our greed, our abuse, our anger. Through example and teaching, Jesus demonstrated that the greatest problems we face and must address in life are issues of the human heart. More than this, Jesus taught that our relationships with others reflect the nature of our relationship with God.

In other words, Jesus wanted us to see that when we are estranged from or angry with one another, it is difficult if not impossible for us to have a healthy relationship with God. "Take care of human relationships first," Jesus was saying, "and then you will be able to take care of your relationship with God. Only after you have made things right with others will you be able to make things right with God." Although this is only one aspect of Jesus's teaching, there are many examples of this theme throughout the Gospels.

Consider, for example, the Lord's Prayer—which many of us, perhaps, pray each week or maybe every day. "Forgive us our trespasses (debts, sins) as we forgive those who trespass against us." What are we asking for when we pray these words? Jesus wanted his disciples to clearly see the relationship between one's willingness to forgive others, and one's ability to receive God's forgiveness. When we say the Lord's Prayer we are affirming our willingness to extend forgiveness to others, and we are expressing that we expect God to extend that same degree of forgiveness to us.

Once, Peter came to Jesus and asked, "Lord, if someone sins against me, how many times should I forgive? Is seven times enough?" (my paraphrase). Jesus answered, "Not just seven times, but seventy times seven" (Matt. 18:21–22). Jesus taught that our human relationships are just as important as our relationship with God. One reflects the other. If we are not whole in our friendships, our families and our communities, God can, and will, seem very distant and removed. The health of our relationships with others reflects the health of our relationship with the Creator.

Jesus also taught such simple concepts as "loving your enemies" (Matt. 5:44), and in his final prayer with the disciples, Jesus prayed that his disciples might be "as one" with one another (John 17:11).

So, what was Jesus getting at? Was he saying that it should be easy for us to love one another, to care for one another and to forgive one another? Quite the contrary. As Jesus understood, human relationships are extraordinarily messy and complex. Even the best marriages have misunderstandings, and a great marriage is built more upon a foundation of hard work and forgiveness than upon some ethereal and fuzzy idea of happiness. Friends can hurt each other. Children can say mean things to their parents. Husbands and wives must rediscover their love and commitment every day. And, I'm sure, if Jesus could have addressed our modern-day situations, he would have had much to say about prejudice, abuse, injustice in the workplace and even road rage!

It would be wonderful, of course, if everyone could get along. But we don't live in that world, do we?

Let's be honest. We all have our favorite friends, our private family circle, our enclave of trustworthy and supportive people who understand us and accept us as we are. For the most part, it is easier for us to love, and get along with, those who love us back.

But we also know those people who—if we had a choice—we'd rather not be around. There are people in our families, in our places of employment, in the classroom, in our churches and maybe people who live across the street from us who are not the easiest to love and accept.

That's why Jesus spent so much time—actually, all of his time—talking about people. He recognized our need. He knew that all of us need healing.

We need relational healing.

We need to know how to get along with one another—especially with those we do not understand or have difficulty accepting and loving. We need God's help if we are to heal the brokenness and heartache in our world.

Likewise, Jesus understood that we are imperfect people. Each of us has problems in our family relationships, in our marriages or with our children that are far less than perfect. We may have situations or difficulties behind closed doors that we feel uncomfortable with or may not have the coping skills to manage effectively. We may have deep-seated anger or animosities that are tearing us apart.

All of us stand in need of God's help and healing when it comes to our relationships. We have a need to open our personal lives—our families, friendships and animosities—to God's healing touch.

As Jesus pointed out, relational healing is a miracle. When our hearts change, *we change.* And without a change of heart, there is no hope for our personal wholeness or the healing of our world.

Surely, one of the greatest miracles we witness every day is when people learn to forgive, to love or to provide for one another. And if we look closely enough, we have all witnessed remarkable acts of charity and forgiveness that call attention to this healing.

Likewise, each of us has probably experienced some form of relational healing in our own lives.

HEALING THE BROKENHEARTED

When Jesus came to the Nazareth synagogue and read from the prophet Isaiah at the beginning of his public ministry, he affirmed that he had come to "bring good news to the poor, to proclaim release to the captives and recovery of sight to the blind, to let the oppressed go free" (Luke 4:18). These are words of healing. But not all of these forms of healing can be readily identified in any outward way. People who are poor or captive or oppressed need God's healing just as much as the person who is blind or deaf. In fact, God's greatest acts of healing are not of the physical variety.

Consider, for example, the needs that exist in your own family, your community, your world—and even in your church. Chances are we know many marriages that are strained to the point of breaking apart. We probably know parents and children who are no longer speaking to each other—or who cannot seem to communicate with each other effectively. There are friendships that have been stressed to the point of resentment. There are communities around our country where people are torn apart or segregated by race, creed, background or station of life. Even a cursory glance at our world reveals that we live in a time that is shot through with anger, animosity and deep desire for revenge. People are hurting everywhere. And there are times when it seems that the world has gone mad with rage.

But there is hope.

The message of Jesus is a message of healing and reconciliation. God desires to heal our divisions, to break down the walls, to bridge the gaps that separate us from one another and, as a result, bring the kingdom into a deeper fullness and visibility in our world. At the very least, God desires that we work toward resolution, understanding and trust—especially with those who disagree with us or who may wish to harm us. Often, through these first steps of reconciliation, we receive the first touch of God's healing in our personal lives.

Not long ago I experienced this need for healing in my own family. My grandfather, who had grown feeble and unable to care for himself, had moved in with my aunt and uncle. As my grandfather's health continued to decline, he also lost some of his personality and willingness to live. In essence, he was preparing himself to die.

Our family—particularly my mother and aunt—found themselves discussing some weighty decisions in regard to my grandfather's long-term care. As a family we would often spend hours
discussing the various possibilities and scenarios that might play
out in the final months of my grandfather's life. There were many
delicate questions to ponder—all relational in nature. Should my
grandfather be moved to a nursing home? Should his house be
sold? How long would my aunt and uncle be able to care for his
needs in their home? What if my grandfather's health took a sudden turn for the worse? Who would care for him then?

These questions brought out many feelings in our family—
both positive and negative. And there were times when the discussions brought out the best in us, revealing the deep love we
had for my grandfather. Likewise, we were forced to seek God's
healing in the midst of this challenging time.

Eventually my mother and aunt decided to admit my grandfather to a nursing facility where he could receive better care.
Although we all knew that my grandfather, well past ninety,
would not be returning to his former self, accepting these
changes was difficult. We had to lean upon God to help us in our
ability to let go—God who would give us wisdom, patience and
respect for one another as we sought the best for my grandfather. Just a few days after my grandfather was admitted to the
home, his health worsened, and he eventually died a very quiet
and peaceful death—a great blessing at the end of a long and
productive life and a marvelous testimony to God's assurance in
times of difficulty.

Every day there are many people who face similar choices and
struggles. Some face far more difficult family decisions. And
many of these choices weigh heavily on our minds and hearts and
can even cause us to experience mental stress or physical illness.
But the real healing work of God must take place in the cracks
and crevices of the relationships themselves. Without the mortar
of wholeness, forgiveness and respect, life grows very bitter and
defeating when we are faced with overwhelming difficulties.

Sometimes we learn to change ourselves. And sometimes, God works through others to bring us this healing.

Take, for example, this beautiful parable, which has its roots in Jewish and Buddhist storytelling. It is one of the most remarkable stories I know about the power of relational healing.

There was a woman who had an only son. One day this son died unexpectedly, leaving this woman heartbroken. For some time she attempted to deal with her grief alone, but she eventually sought out a healer to help her in her grief.

"I know a remedy for grief," the healer told her. "Bring me a mustard seed from a home that has never known sorrow and you will be healed."

Right away the woman set off on her journey, going from house to house in her search for the magic seed. At the first house, she met a man who appeared to be rather well-to-do, and she assumed that her search may be over. "If you would be so kind," the woman said. "I'm searching for a seed from a house that has never known sorrow."

"You won't find it here," the man replied. "My wife died a few months ago, and I have been lost ever since."

At the next house, the woman encountered a neighbor who felt sick at heart because she had grown estranged from a dear friend. Another house revealed a woman who had recently endured a painful divorce. "No magic seeds here," they explained. "We have known our share of suffering."

And so it went. In house after house the woman found that everyone had experienced some form of loss or sorrow. She talked to them. She shared the mysteries of her soul.

In time, the woman grew to appreciate her new friends, and forgot about her search for the magic seed. She never returned to the healer, and day by day, her grief and sorrow melted away.

IMAGES OF HEALING

God desires to heal us in this way. Our relationships are the most important aspect of life itself. And when our relationships are sick, we are sick.

Perhaps that is the reason why Jesus spent so much time talking about the ways we relate to one another, and why it is vitally important for us to be whole in our relationships with one another before we can be whole in our relationship with God.

We all stand in need of this healing. We need reminders of this healing power. And we need to see God's healing reflected in our lives.

Perhaps one of the most powerful images of this healing can be seen in the movie, *Places in the Heart*. This movie, starring Sally Field, portrays the struggles of a Southern widow whose husband has been killed by a young black man. In order to make ends meet and save the family farm, the widow takes on two tenants—a blind man who has been ostracized from his family and a black sharecropper (played by Danny Glover). The movie portrays the struggles of these people and the special bonds of understanding and friendship (maybe even bonds of "family") that they form.

At the end of the film, there is a very moving scene in the church. The choir rises to sing "In the Garden," and the pastor begins to explain the significance of communion as the trays containing the bread and cup are passed from pew to pew and from person to person. We see the widow sitting next to her children, offering them the bread and saying, "Peace of God." The children offer the elements to the blind man, who turns to offer God's peace to the black sharecropper. The sharecropper turns to offer Christ's love to a leader of the community who is also a closet Klansman.

Suddenly, we inexplicably see the widow's dead husband sitting in the pew. He accepts the body and blood of Christ, then turns to offer the same to the young black man who had shot him. "Peace of God," he says. "Peace of God," the young man replies.

This movie hints at a truth that Jesus himself talked about. That is, without the reconciling love of God in our lives, we are nothing. The greatest healing work of God occurs in the places of the human heart.

What do you think? Does God heal us? Does God want to? The scriptures affirm that this is God's greatest desire. This is the central message of Christ—that he came to reconcile and make new, to restore that which was broken, to forgive, to love and to redeem that which was lost.

If there are broken relationships in our lives, we can rest assured that God desires to mend them. God desires that we learn to care for one another, to make the best of our situations and our failures. This is, of course, the most difficult work of all. We don't always want what God wants. Sometimes bitterness, envy, jealousy and anger get in the way of God's healing.

Often, we wonder: what hope is there?

Perhaps the deepest glimpse of God's relational healing may be found in the final days that Jesus shared with those he loved. During his final hours, Jesus gave the disciples two important images of reconciliation. One of these—Holy Communion or the Lord's Supper—we know very well. The image of Jesus sharing his body and blood with his disciples is most important. Here we discover the way that we relate to God, and God relates to us.

In the Lord's Supper, we are the recipients. God is the giver. All we can do is accept what God offers. This is called grace. There is nothing we can do to *earn* God's gift of salvation. In other words, when it comes to our relationship with God, we are on unequal ground. There is nothing we can do to claim equality with God. Communion is a reminder that God is the giver and we are the recipients. Through Communion, God shares with us.

But in the Gospel of John, we find another act that Jesus asked his disciples to share with one another. Here, in John 13, Jesus takes a basin of water and a towel and washes the disciples' feet. Peter protests, but then Jesus explains: "If I, your Lord and Teacher, have washed your feet, you also ought to wash one another's feet" (John 13:14).

The idea of washing one another's feet has to do with relational healing. Service, humility and sacrifice are important in this act, as it is important in all of our relationships. When we place ourselves first in the scheme of things, or when we forget the needs of others, we refuse to wash one another's feet. Jesus wanted to remind the disciples that, just as the bread and wine are important for our understanding of how God relates to us, the basin and towel are important for our understanding of how we are to relate to one another.

These images and practices are important. Without them, we can easily forget how needy we are, and how much we need to be healed of our brokenness and confusion. So many of life's difficulties and problems fade away when we find reconciliation with one another, learn how to sacrifice for one another, and learn how to work, play and pray together. So many of the world's most perplexing and maddening threats could be put to rest if we allowed God's healing to break through our hearts and change how we relate to one another. After all, most of the biggest problems we face are actually very close to home.

So often, people are lonely because they have no one who cares for them—or because they refuse to reach out to others. People are often angry because they have not known love and unconditional acceptance. Children are often conflicted when parents are not there to guide them. Others grow up to be violent because they were ignored or abused. Marriages break apart when there is infidelity, mistrust, lack of communication or lack of love. Many people are hungry, but it is our human apathy, our conflicts and our unwillingness to share that is most often at the heart of human hunger—not a lack of food supply or ability to feed.

Without exception, all of these are relational issues. And without exception, the most difficult work we do in life is relational in nature: learning how to love and support the people we love, and learning how to accept and love the people who cause us conflict and distress.

But God wants to help us. God is the healer. And often God's greatest work of healing begins in us and within the people we see every day. God can teach us, also, how to heal one another and how to give one another what we need.

We can experience this healing. We can learn to be healers. And the healing can begin the moment we realize our need for God's help, just like the psalmist who once prayed:

Incline your ear, O Lord, and answer me, for I am poor and
    needy.
Preserve my life, for I am devoted to you; save your servant
    who trusts in you.
You are my God; be gracious to me, O Lord, for to you do I cry
    all day long.
Gladden the soul of your servant, for to you, O Lord, I lift up
    my soul.
For you, O Lord, are good and forgiving, abounding in steadfast
    love to all who call on you.
Give ear, O Lord, to my prayer; listen to my cry of supplication.
In the day of my trouble I call on you, for you will answer me.
    (Ps. 86:1–7)

1
STUDY GUIDE

The author begins his exploration of healing by first looking at our relationships and how our human connections
can be a source of health or distress in our lives. Consider
your own relationships—your family, friendships, coworkers
and neighbors. Take a few moments to reflect on the health
of these relationships in your life, then move to the following questions.

- What questions come to mind when you think of
  healing?
- Why do you think the author began with relational
  healing and our need to be whole and reconciled
  people?
- How is relational healing, and our human need,
  reflected in the scriptures?
- What do you think of the author's assessment that
  most of the pain and misery in our lives is connected
  with human relationships?
- What types of relational stresses might indicate a need
  for healing (loneliness, depression, etc.)?
- Consider the parable of the grieving woman and the
  magic seed. What lessons about healing can be drawn
  from this story?

Read Matthew 5:23–24 as well as other portions of
Matthew 5–7. What types of relational problems does Jesus
address? How could these problems be healed with human

intervention or God's help? What, in your estimation, are some of the larger human difficulties facing our world today? In what ways are mended lives healed lives?

Prayer: Creator God, who formed us and gave us one another to love and appreciate, we ask you to assist us in our fear, our loneliness, our hatred and our apathy. You give us many opportunities to help one another and to be a blessing to the world each day of our lives. Heal our brokenness, we pray, and change our hardened hearts into receptive dwelling places of your Spirit. Make us whole. And free us for joyful obedience. Amen.

CHAPTER 2

Spiritual Healing: Dealing with the Emptiness Inside Us

As [Jesus] was getting into the boat, the man who had been possessed by demons begged him that he might be with him. But Jesus refused, and said to him, "Go home to your friends, and tell them how much the Lord has done for you, and what mercy he has shown you." And he went away and began to proclaim in the Decapolis how much Jesus had done for him; and everyone was amazed.

—Mark 5:18–20

*D*uring my college years, I participated in a makeshift jail ministry of prayer and Bible study sponsored by the Gideon's Bible society. Every Thursday evening I would meet two or three older gentlemen at a local restaurant where we would carpool to the county lockup—a jail that was, at that time, considered the most deplorable of its kind in the entire state. I would not have disagreed with that assessment.

The county jail was an old, dilapidated structure filled with vermin and roaches. Inside, long rows of tiny cells lined either side of a common area where the inmates ate and socialized at picnic tables. A solitary lightbulb hung from the ceiling, casting an eerie glow across this depressing landscape of graffiti and iron. The scent of sweat and urine hung in the air like a fog.

As you might imagine, visiting the men in this jail was anything but a pleasant experience. In fact, it was rather depressing and at times, frightening.

I recall that, during one of these visits, another leader and I were led to an upstairs cell designed for solitary confinement—a place the sheriff's department reserved for the most hardened of criminals. We were told that, behind the door, a man was waiting to speak to us. The sheriff removed a key from his pocket and unlocked a small, bar-lined opening—the only portal through which the inmate could interact with visitors. We peered inside.

There, lying on a makeshift cot, we saw the visage of a large, burly man whose body was practically covered with a long mane of graying hair. When my friend spoke, the man rose to his feet and lumbered over to greet us. We introduced ourselves, but kept our distance.

"Who did you say you are?" the inmate asked at one point.

"We come here every Thursday to have prayer with the fellas," my friend explained.

"I don't pray," the man explained.

"We could pray for you," I countered. "Or if you have family—a wife or children who might need some extra help—we could try to offer assistance."

The man stared blankly at us through dark eyes, hair tucked and twisted around his bearded mouth. "What I want," he said eventually—with more than a touch of animosity and loathing—"is to be left alone." And with that word, he stretched his fingers through the bars and clanked the portal door shut.

Although it was a long time ago now, the image of that solitary man behind the steel door is still vivid in my memory. From time to time, I wonder what happened to him. I wonder if he was released from jail or is now serving time in a federal or state prison. I wonder if he is alive or dead.

The image of that solitary man—secluded and shut off from the world, kept behind bars like a caged animal—has become something of a metaphor to me as well. There are days when I think I have met him in some of the lonely, defeated and downtrodden people I encounter. I often see his face again in the spiritually dry countenances of people who have given up on life or their families or their futures and have chosen to live in a spiritual seclusion, far from the goodness and peace of God. The man behind the bars could be you or me, even—in those moments when we decide to close our hearts or minds and isolate ourselves from God or others.

I think of this man, too, every time I read the biblical account of the tormented soul who lived among the tombstones of the Gerasenes (Mark 5:1–20). This story, one of the most compelling and uplifting stories found anywhere in the Gospels, is rich with spiritual significance and insights about the healing touch of God.

Here was a man who, we are told, had an "unclean spirit"—a man whose rage could only be suppressed with chains and shackles, a man who howled at the moon and bruised himself with stones. In one of the most graphic depictions to be found anywhere in the scriptures, this man is portrayed as being spiritually "dead"—having no hope for redemption, cut off and isolated from all that gives life and hope and purpose. But Jesus enters into his world and changes his life forever.

Perhaps one of the reasons why the Gospel writer paints such a graphic portrait of this tormented soul is simply this: so we who read the story can understand the parallels and innuendoes directed at our own lives and the world in which we live. This, indeed, is one of the ways in which the Gospel touches us. For clearly, we can see ourselves living among the tombs of this age.

Consider, for example, how much death there is in our world today, and how much these images of death affect us (subliminally, subconsciously and otherwise). We have witnessed the death of thousands in a single moment (September 11), and read almost daily of suicidal bombings, racial or ethnic "cleansing" where scores of people are slaughtered mercilessly, and see via satellite the images of sadness and suffering found in the aftermath of such destruction. Is it not entirely possible that many people (yes, even those in the church) are living in a spiritually "dead" manner where it is easier to carry on among the tombs and simply turn a blind eye to the death and destruction that is all around us? In time, we simply become numb to these excesses, and eventually, quite unaware of our environs and the need we have for God's intervention.

This, I believe, is the ultimate message of the Gerasenes. We are people living among the tombs, and if we open our eyes, we can see the rage and anger seething through our world and all of the chains we attempt to design to keep this rage under control. But it is difficult to come out of the cemetery and enter into life. And so, as Jesus taught, we prefer to wage war on one another, to kill one another in real and in spiritual ways (Matt. 5:21–26; Matt. 5:38–48) rather than to accept God's plan for our world and embrace the new life and new order that God has to offer.

We know much about the Gerasenes. We see this reflected in our music, our literature and our art.

In his 1990s song, "The End of the Innocence," Don Henley wrote eloquently about "people filled with rage." Other songs of that time revealed a growing disillusionment among the young.

And today we see how hatred has become a symbol for our time, as we now speak of "road rage" or "workplace rage" as if they are everyday occurrences. This anger has also come full circle in our schools, in our political conversations, and in the growing disparity between those who have and those who have not. Theater and art have also revealed this human search for meaning and purpose and the spiritual disillusionment of our time. The movie, *Forrest Gump,* has several poignant moments where we see the spiritual death of the individual and our world exposed and then brought to life again. One of these scenes takes place at sea, when Forrest and Lieutenant Dan are fishing for shrimp.

Forrest, the main character of the movie, has always approached life with a simple faith in God and an unwavering trust and love for others—especially for his beloved Jenny and the angry Lieutenant Dan, who lost his legs in the Vietnam War. Though both Jenny and Lieutenant Dan have rejected Forrest's friendship and love on numerous occasions, Forrest has remained faithful to them over the years. Forrest had even named his shrimp boat "Jenny," and had taken on Lieutenant Dan as his first mate in an effort to redeem them from their lost condition and keep them close to his heart.

Eventually, a great storm serves as the backdrop for a showdown between Lieutenant Dan and God—where the Vietnam vet hangs from the mast (as if lifted on a cross) and shouts into the angry storm, "This is it! It's either you or me!"

When the storm subsides, Forrest and Lieutenant Dan have survived to shrimp another day (after the entire Louisiana shrimp fleet is wiped out), and their fortunes are made. Then, on a bright and beautiful day at sea, we witness one of the turning points in the movie, when Lieutenant Dan—finally released from the haunting chains of his bitter past—lets go of his anger and thanks Forrest for saving his life in Vietnam. As Lieutenant Dan suddenly falls joyously over the side of the boat and swims toward the gleaming light of the sun sparkling upon the water, we hear Forrest saying, "Now, he never said so, but I think he made his peace with God."

Such images help us to see more clearly our need for spiritual healing, and also help us to recognize that there are spiritual dimensions to life that, unless nurtured and tended, become dark and angry places of the soul.

Indeed, there are many people filled with rage in our world. Each day we go to work with people who are bound with chains of depression, perhaps, or chains of hopelessness or chains of greed. We sit next to people in the classroom who live among the tombs of abuse and dreary existence. Likewise, there are many who may put on a smile in the morning, but may go to bed at night weeping in chains of loneliness and despair.

But the story of the Gerasenes does not end with the chains. The drama does not reach denouement in the cemetery.

Like so many accounts in the Gospels and elsewhere in the writings of St. Paul, we are told that God can touch us and heal us of our spiritual infirmities.

The man of the Gerasenes, we are told, had an unclean spirit that tormented him. And indeed, there are many unclean spirits that can be unleashed in our lives, too.

Consider, for example, all of the people who are plagued by the unclean spirit of alcoholism or drug addiction or habit. Others are kept in chains by spirits of lust or greed or ego. Still others suffer from the tormented spirit of abuse or hatred or nihilism. These spirits fill our world. We can see their power and sway over human life every day.

As the apostle once wrote, "For our struggle is not against enemies of blood and flesh, but against the rulers, against the authorities, against the cosmic powers of this present darkness, against the spiritual forces of evil" (Eph. 6:12).

Surprisingly, however, we rarely speak of spiritual healing—though at its core, this is what the message of the Gospel addresses most powerfully. The needs of humanity are not so much physical and social in nature as they are spiritual. As John

Wesley, whose revival once changed the face of England and America in the late 1700s, once noted, the need of "heart change" is ever before us.

These metaphors of "heart," "will" and "mind"—as used both scripturally and in the language of theologians and reformers through the ages—point most specifically to matters of the spirit. And spirit, of course, is the realm of God. Spirit is also the place, more wonderfully and fully, where God meets us, redeems us and loves us.

This is spiritual healing. This is transformation. Hope. Joy. Salvation.

HEALING IS EVERY STEP

Another personal story might help to illustrate the nature of spiritual healing and what it can mean for us today.

Some years ago, a young lady approached me after a worship service (I'll call her Sue) and asked if she could speak to me. She seemed at once both strangely joyous and bothered—as if she had made some momentous breakthrough in her life, but didn't know what to make of it.

"I'm visiting here for the first time," she told me. "It's been a long time since I've been in a church."

"That's interesting," I said. "And what brought you here today? Did someone invite you?"

"No," she answered. "I've driven by this church many times. But there was something that kept tugging at me. I'm not sure what. Just a feeling of emptiness, I think. Maybe a feeling that there is supposed to be more to this life than I can explain."

"And so you walked in today," I said.

"That's right," she answered. "I was driving by and this time, I stopped. When I came in and sat down, you were talking about Christ's table—"

"—Communion," I said. "The Lord's Supper."

"Yes, and I heard you say that Christ himself was inviting me to this table, that he would accept me as I am and that God loved us even while we were yet sinners."

I waited for her to continue.

"I've had many hardships in my life," she explained. "My step-father abused me when I was a little girl, and I've never felt very worthy to be in the presence of God. I think my past has colored most everything I do and has affected my relationships and my self-esteem. But I think I'm willing to accept that God could love someone like me."

A lump gathered in my throat. How amazing, I thought, that this woman had gone through her life feeling unloved and unwanted, but had walked into the church, cold turkey, and experienced the love of God. Not only did Sue accept Communion that day when the invitation was given, but later she attended a new member's class, where she explored her faith more deeply and was eventually baptized into the Christian faith.

Since that time, I have met many people like Sue who have experienced a spiritual healing in their lives. It is as if they have come out of the tombs of despair into a new life.

Such transformations, however, are not always so profound or sudden, and many of the transformations in our lives come to us when we are able to accept our own limitations, sins or failures. So often, spiritual vitality comes when we are able to change our focus in life, or perhaps come to recognize that there is a higher power that can lift us up, fill us with purpose and enable us to change and grow into goodness.

This is really what the twelve-step program designed by Alcoholics Anonymous is devised to do. One step comes when a person is able to admit that there is a problem, and that he cannot overcome this problem on his own. A second step is a willingness to accept that there is a "higher power," and that this power is needed to overcome the addiction.

Although twelve-step programs were originally designed to help heal people with alcohol addiction, similar programs have been used successfully to help people with many other problems, such as food addictions or other uncontrolled cravings. But at the heart of these programs there is a recognition that our physical and emotional problems are rooted in spiritual need.

This understanding is a key component to our health—not just physically, but relationally, emotionally and in every other way. Our spiritual healing will always precede any type of bodily healing or change of direction or focus in life. And that is one of the reasons why I have placed this chapter earlier in the book.

God's healing touch is a spiritual touch. And the largest problems that you and I face in life are always, at heart, spiritual in nature.

As I ponder, for example, my wife's recovery from breast cancer, I am struck by the ways in which each of us turned to God. Long before there was a physical healing (before treatments, surgery or recuperation), there were prayers, deep conversations of the heart, the joining of our thoughts for my wife's full recovery. These were spiritual steps, and they preceded the actual physical ones.

A quick glance at several other "healings" in the Bible might also reveal the true nature of spiritual healing and what it can mean for us.

Consider the story of King Hezekiah's healing as recorded in 2 Kings 20. Here was a good king who had fallen ill—"to the point of death" (20:1)—and was not expected to recover. When the prophet Isaiah came to visit, he did not offer an encouraging word to the king (much like a patient might receive the bad news of a doctor's diagnosis). "You're not going to make it," Isaiah told him.

And what was Hezekiah's response? He reacted in several ways—much like most people would when faced with such bleak and disturbing news. Hezekiah turned all of his energy inward, turned away from the bad news and prayed to God (20:2). Later, he wept, cleansing himself of the bitterness and anger he must have felt (20:3). He asked for God's healing (20:4).

What is significant about Hezekiah's story is not so much the fact that he was healed physically (Isaiah later returned to inform the king that he would live for a few more years), but that he walked through the steps of grief and questioning that is part and parcel of all serious illness. The spiritual quest preceded the physical.

It is also worth noting that Hezekiah eventually died. I point this out because, so often, when people think of healing, they overlook the fact that physical health is fleeting. All of us owe God a death, and there is nothing that we will do, or can do, to weasel out of this reality.

Much of our talk of healing breaks down at exactly this point. So often we overlook the fact that the essence of all healing is spiritual in nature. A person who has been healed of a broken back through the conventional means of surgery and rehabilitation will eventually wither and die. Likewise, the person who walks onto an auditorium stage, tosses down the crutches and says, "I'm healed," will someday be bedridden once again and will eventually die.

I have known doctors who could not speak to their patients about these realities, as well as pastors and chaplains who will never speak of death with a seriously ill or dying person. Well-known faith healers and televangelists who offer the laying on of hands as a cure for all maladies are equally unwilling to accept these human ends, and offer a lopsided presentation of healing that is both silent and damaging. Few, if any of them, ever speak of death before their audiences.

Sometimes spiritual healing can come about only when we understand fully and completely that we are going to die. Our lives are finite. Our days are numbered. No amount of laying on of hands and prayer will *ultimately* keep a human body from breaking down. But we will discuss the hope of these matters in another chapter.

Ultimately, coming to an understanding of our own demise is not a depressing realization, but a life-freeing, life-giving thing. The realities of death point us to each other—and to the life-giving hope of learning how to care for each other—and, of course, to God, who is ultimately our hope and salvation. If we had the abilities to expand our lives and live forever, we would, of course, have no need of God. We would be immortal.

But the scriptures remind us that our days are like grass and that we shall all wither and perish like the flowers of the field (Ps. 90:5–6). We can, however, experience abundant life—a life filled with joy and wonder and promise. This is the spiritual healing that Jesus spoke about.

In the Gospel of Luke, Jesus enters his hometown synagogue and offers a design for his ministry, which he reveals from the prophet Isaiah. Amazingly, this picture of ministry includes a healing touch and the promise of transformed life. What Jesus read were these words: "The Spirit of the Lord is upon me, because he has anointed me to bring good news to the poor. He has sent me to proclaim release to the captives and recovery of sight to the blind, to let the oppressed go free, to proclaim the year of the Lord's favor" (Luke 4:18–19).

These metaphors—rich in power and significance—speak to the spiritual needs of our existence as much as our physical ones, and maybe more so. A transformed life is a great miracle of God. Hope in the midst of suffering is a spiritual work. And there are types of blindness that have nothing to do with the eyes.

When we speak of healing in the church, we must not neglect the work of the Spirit, who has come to heal our brokenness, our hatred, our apathy, our greed, our weariness and our animosities. When fear has been displaced with faith, we are healed. When depression and loneliness is displaced by hope, there is a healing.

In fact, the Spirit's work is relentless.

We witness spiritual healing every day.

2
STUDY GUIDE

Spiritual healing is evident in both the Bible and our personal lives. And yet, we are often oblivious to God's ongoing work and the healing that is taking place in the broken, hopeless and despairing places of our world. Take a few moments to reflect upon these matters—both in personal and educational ways—and then proceed to the questions.

- In what ways might our spiritual condition affect our health—positively or negatively?
- How might spiritual disease be reflected in our emotions, our relationships or our bodies?
- How might our spiritual health precede our physical well-being?
- Why do you think we find it so difficult to speak about the realities of death—in spite of the universal reality of the human condition?
- What do you think of the author's assertion that spiritual transformations are healings? The idea that spiritual questions and struggles always precede physical transformations?

Read any or all of the following scripture passages: 2 Kings 20; Matthew 5:21–26, 38–48; Ephesians 6:12; Luke 4:18–19. Then ask: What spiritual realities are being expressed in these passages? How do these passages reflect the spiritual realities of our lives and our need to be healed? What lessons can be drawn from these passages about the need for spiritual healing in my life?

Prayer: Holy Spirit, come and transform us. Save us from cheap faith and easy grace. Help us to open our eyes that we may see those dead and dying places in our lives and our need for spiritual renewal. Heal our wounded spirits and save us from those spiritual trials that destroy our faith, or worse, cause us to destroy the faith of others. We want to be let loose from our chains. Heal *my spirit,* Lord. Amen.

CHAPTER 3

Emotional Healing:
Faithfully Honoring Our Feelings

*And he came to Nazareth, where he had been brought
up: and, as his custom was, he went into the synagogue
on the Sabbath day, and stood up for to read. And there
was delivered unto him the book of the prophet Isaiah.
And when he had opened the book, he found the place
where it was written, the Spirit of the Lord is upon me,
because he hath anointed me to preach the gospel to
the poor; he hath sent me to heal the brokenhearted,
to preach deliverance to the captives, and recovering
of sight to the blind, to set at liberty them that are
bruised, to preach the acceptable year of the Lord.*

—Luke 4:16–19, KJV

*T*he nuances of God's healing touch are not only reflected in life itself, but also in the Bible. I have chosen this passage from Luke—and from the King James Version—because there is a particular phrase that weighs heavily in our consideration of God's healing touch, particularly in regard to our emotional health.

The King James Version of this passage records that, when Jesus offered himself as a fulfillment of the prophet Isaiah's vision of ministry, he said that he had come to "heal the brokenhearted."

I appreciate this little nuance of language very much, for it offers hope in a heartbroken world. Each day we need to be reminded that the things that break our hearts are also the things that break the heart of God. Our life experiences are not estranged from the One who made us, from the One who offers us strength and assurance in every time of need.

Moreover, we were created with emotions. God gave us the capacity to experience love, anger, fear, anxiety, contentment and joy, among many other emotions. In fact, every day of our lives is overflowing with feeling. We are swept up in emotion, for example, when we face a weighty decision, a sudden change of circumstance or a horrible turn that threatens to undo us. We can also be swept up—in good ways and bad—into feelings of ecstasy, celebration, passion or awe. Our emotional state can lift us up or press us down. There are times when our feelings make good moments greater, and times when our feelings can make minor difficulties or worries seem insurmountable. Our emotions affect so much of what we do—how we act, how we respond to others and how we treat ourselves.

Consider, for example, how the loss of a job can affect us emotionally. At first there may be bitterness and anger toward the boss or the company. Later, these ill feelings that we have directed at others may turn inward, leaving us in a wake of depression, anxiety or self-loathing. Many people who have lost a job find themselves sleeping more and eating less. Others may sleep less and eat more. Regardless, without proper healing, these emotions can eat away at our health—leaving us overweight or sick or even on the brink of heart attack or ulcer. Many destructive habits, such as smoking or drinking to excess, often follow on the heels of life-altering events—such as a job loss, a death in the family or a new position that demands far more than we have to give.

This same emotional roller coaster can be seen in teenagers when a boyfriend or girlfriend breaks off a relationship. We can see the emotional stresses brought about by a change of school and moving to a new city, by the death of a friend, by insurmountable debt or by unresolved abuses of the past. Some adults cannot shake themselves loose from mistakes they have made, or from regrets that haunt or color all of their future actions. Others are eaten up by jealousy or envy. Still others may have unresolved anger that is directed at an ex-spouse, a parent (living or dead) or a group of people (whether known or faceless).

There are so many events and changes in life that can affect our emotional health and stability. And there are so many moments that can break our hearts.

But there is good news. God can heal our emotions. God can help us to overcome the feelings of loss, bitterness, anger or envy. God can take what is broken and mend it.

HEALTH AND HONESTY

In his bestselling book, *The Road Less Traveled,* M. Scott Peck begins with a chapter entitled "Problems and Pain." His insights here are simple, yet profound, and the first sentence contains only three words: Life is difficult.[2]

Scott Peck observes that so many of our problems are built upon the faulty expectation that life should, somehow, be easy for us. We so often live with the belief that problems are not intrinsic to life, and should not, therefore, affect us. Or we may operate with the idea that, while others may experience problems and pain, we should somehow be immune to life's random difficulties. And so we moan and groan about life's small injustices, minor offenses and tiny setbacks—bringing ourselves to believe that these difficulties are insurmountable, or that we should be free to solve our problems without experiencing any form of discomfort or pain.

These expectations, of course, are not true to life. They are not based on reality. The fact is, each of us will experience difficulties, setbacks, challenges and pain. But the difference in how people learn to deal with these problems can be found in forms of discipline: what we believe about a problem, how we choose to feel about it and the choices we make in overcoming life's demands.

Without doubt, our emotional health plays a vital role in our ability to face life's challenges with confidence and victory. Our emotional health plays a large role in our performance as human beings—how well we work, how well we play, how well we relate to others, and the manner in which we receive from and give back to our families, our communities and our friends.

Our emotional health and outlook is also vital to our bodily health. Healing after a surgery, or in the wake of other serious illness, is often speeded by the positive and focused emotions of the patient and family. A person who *feels* good, who has a resilient emotional strength, is going to recover more rapidly than a person who is fearful or anxious, or who gives up on life (if that person recovers at all).

Life is difficult—but God desires to heal our damaged emotions as much as God desires to touch a bruised body. I've seen evidences of this truth on many occasions.

During my seminary years, I served as a chaplain in a large university hospital. The experience there was grueling and challenging for a young pastor like me, to say the least. But in that setting, I learned so much about people and about the connections between our feelings and our bodies.

Some of the most obvious connections I witnessed, however, were not always found among the patients themselves, but also among the hospital staff. In fact, there were times when I found myself spending as much time with the nurses and doctors who worked my floor as I did among the patients they served.

I noted, for example, that some of the nurses on that floor went about their routines with an attitude of helpfulness and lightness. It was clear that they approached their work seriously, but also with a sense of their own limitations and an awareness of their personal needs. These were the nurses that always had the ability to laugh during an otherwise traumatic experience. These nurses also maintained an uncanny ability to comfort a grieving family with just the right word.

Their emotional stability and outlook reminded me so much of the fictional character of Hawkeye Pierce—the leg-slapping, cutup of a surgeon who was the central figure in the hit television show *M*A*S*H*. Like these nurses, Hawkeye had the ability to keep himself and others focused on the unexpected joys and healing possibilities amid the atrocities and dejections of working in a MASH unit during the Korean War. Even in the surgery room, Hawkeye took it upon himself to keep the mood light and to focus attention on matters other than the suffering at hand. In one episode, I recall Hawkeye offering his personal philosophy to a new doctor by saying something like, "You can't let yourself get too close to other people's misery, otherwise, you may never be able to climb out of that misery yourself."

People like Mother Teresa and St. Francis have also made similar observations about life's difficulties. We cannot be healers of others until we have been wounded and healed ourselves. Our vitality and helpfulness to others often depends on our own emotional health.

Most of the nurses of that hospital wing embodied this reality—but not all. Unlike those nurses that went about their duties with a self-awareness and helpful spirit, others, I observed, seemed crushed and distraught by the constant realities of their dying patients or by the stresses and demands they brought with them to the hospital. There were nurses who seemed distracted by anger or despair. Some could not function well at their jobs because of situations at home—where emotional circumstances weighed heavily on their minds. Others guarded their feelings and would not speak of their patients. Some avoided family members that they passed in the hallways and rarely offered a hopeful word to them about their loved ones.

Like the patients they were serving, the people who worked in the hospital were filled with the same emotional wounds and deep needs as those lying in the hospital beds. I was glad that I learned this lesson early on in my ministry, for it has saved me much heartache and misery. Life is difficult—and we must be aware of our own emotional state and our emotional needs if we are to become whole people. And if we are to be of help to others, then our emotional state must be far more resilient yet.

Certainly, this is true for each of us, and a healthy faith recognizes this reality.

Consider, for example, how often Jesus spoke of our emotional state. "Blessed are those who mourn, for they will be comforted" is more than just a statement about sorrow (Matt. 5:4). Jesus was making clear that mourning is an essential process in our healing. When we feel a loss, our mourning is the avenue through which God enters our lives and heals us. Tears are cleansing and without them, we cannot let go of the pain and experience God's healing touch.

Jesus also talked much about anger, fear, hope, joy and despair. He affirmed that our tears (as well as our laughter) are healing.

Not all people understand this, however. There have been times when I have seen people deny their sorrow—as if tears or sadness are somehow the antithesis to faith—and refuse to cry at a funeral. I have even heard some say that a Christian is not supposed to mourn, since a true faith is always hopeful.

This is not only a stark misrepresentation of the Christian faith, but a denial of how Jesus himself taught and lived. Jesus wept over his friend Lazarus. Jesus felt the pangs of separation from friends; he also experienced loneliness, heartache and sadness. He wept deeply in Gethsemane as he faced the prospect of a cruel cross.

To believe that our emotions aren't real, or that we should somehow suppress them, is a denial of our true, created selves. Believing that emotions are evil is a denial of God's work. Jesus himself experienced many emotions. And so do we. It should be noted that Jesus was angry when he drove out the people who were conducting business in the temple (Mark 11:15–17).

In the Gospels, Jesus is also portrayed as having experienced grief (John 11:35, Matt. 26:37), frustration (John 12:7–8), compassion (Matt. 15:32), disappointment (Matt. 26:50) and anguish (Matt. 26:39), among many other feelings. Indeed, we can be assured that, just as Jesus was created and tested in all respects as we are (Heb. 4:15), he must have experienced the full range of emotions, passions, insecurities and doubts that we all do.

But unlike us, Jesus learned how to master his emotions and lived a life completed by faithfulness and sacrifice.

When we are angry, for example, we often allow that emotion to overtake us, dictating what we say, how we act or how we treat others—usually thinking of ourselves first. Instead of expressing our anger in a helpful manner, as Jesus did, we often speak words we cannot take back, or strike out in ways that are counterproductive to both our needs and the needs of others. Or perhaps our anger quakes into a mountain of hatred or into full-blown prejudice or violence. Our world is filled with daily evidences of people who cannot control their rage, people who refuse to allow their emotional wounds to be healed.

Good anger is expressed when we see injustice and speak up about it. God gave us anger so that we could help to right the wrongs of the world, so that we could find within us the strength and attitude that we often need to take a stand and make the necessary changes in our society and our world.

Looking at these realities more deeply, and more personally, we can see that most often God's healing comes when we are able to forgive or make amends or express our pain to a person who has wronged us. Some of God's greatest gifts come to us at the point of our pain—healing our brokenness, our anger or our greed. God's healing comes in the form of justice—when old animosities are laid to rest or offered up in restitution to those who have been hurt—and peace comes at last. Or God's healing may also come in the simple ability to lay aside those things that weigh us down (desire for material goods, for example), replacing these desires with contentment or a simplified lifestyle.

There is no doubt that God can heal our emotional wounds.

But we can also learn how to turn away from destructive patterns and find help through a variety of disciplines that can help us tap into God's healing mercy.

Prayer is one of the classic disciplines of faith—but so often we don't see the connection between prayer and our healed emotions. When we turn our attentions inward, or focus our desires more squarely upon God and neighbor, our attitudes do change. Other people might find that meditative practices—focusing on scripture recitation or patterned thoughts—works well. Talking to a family member about our pain, or with a trusted friend, is another time-tested method of healing.

It should also be noted that when we are depressed or hurting, we do not always feel like praying—or perhaps we simply can't bring ourselves to focus attention on anything other than our own misery. Many of the Psalms reflect this feeling. For example, the psalmist once prayed, "I am poured out like water . . . my strength is dried up . . . You have brought me down to the dust of the earth" (Ps. 22:14–15, my paraphrase from KJV). Psalm 69 says, "The waters have swept over my soul . . . and I am weary of crying" (vv. 1–3) and "I have looked for some to take pity, but have found none; and for comforters, but have found none" (vs. 20, my paraphrase from KJV).

These times—when our despair covers us or when we find it difficult or impossible to pray—are not times when we are apart from God, however. Rather, God is all the nearer to us. As the apostle Paul affirmed in his letter to the Romans: "Likewise the Spirit helps us in our weakness; for we do not know how to pray as we ought, but that very Spirit intercedes with sighs too deep for words. And God, who searches the heart, knows what is the mind of the Spirit, because the Spirit intercedes for the saints according to the will of God" (Rom. 8:26–27).

Knowing that there will be times when we cannot pray, or times when we may feel dejected or apathetic, it is helpful to prepare for such moments when we are on top of life. I have found it helpful to prepare for these times in my life by keeping a box of affirmations stashed away. These affirmations are notes, cards and awards that I have received from others. They may be Christmas cards from old friends or birthday cards with sentimental poems written inside them. Some are letters from my wife or children, often with photographs. Many of these affirmations are from people in the congregations I have served—notes and letters affirming my ministry, thanking me for my help or my prayers or simply expressing gratitude to God. So whenever I feel like I am losing hope, I take out a few of these affirmations and read them. Amazingly, I am reminded of other people's love, and I feel a new surge of energy.

Keeping these kinds of affirmations close at hand are important, I believe, because as human beings we are far more influenced by the negative than the positive. I once heard a psychologist say that for every negative comment or complaint we hear, it takes ten affirmations or positive words to lift us. That's ten to one! All the more reason to keep a few emotional pick-me-ups on hand. We never know when we might need them.

Other people may find that carrying a written prayer in a purse or wallet can also be helpful. Often, when I find myself in need of an emotional lift, or when I am suffering due to feelings that I cannot shake lose from my heart (such as anger, despair or apathy), I pray the prayer of St. Francis. This prayer is a reminder that God's work can take place within our outlook and attitude. When we pray for a change of heart (which is also a change of feeling), God's presence can make us whole.

The prayer of St. Francis is a simple prayer, yet deeply helpful to all who experience emotional turmoil.

> Lord, make me an instrument of thy peace.
> Where there is hatred, let me sow love;
> Where there is injury, pardon;
> Where there is doubt, faith;
> Where there is despair, hope;
> Where there is darkness, light;
> Where there is sadness, joy;
> O divine Master, grant that I may not so much seek
> To be consoled as to console,
> To be understood as to understand,
> To be loved as to love,
> For it is in giving that we receive;
> It is in pardoning that we are pardoned;
> It is dying that we are born to eternal life.

I hope you find this prayer helpful also, but if not, keep another prayer on hand that will encourage you in a time of despair. Write down your thoughts during the high moments of your life, or keep a journal of your experiences that you can reread during the low moments.

By preparing for life's bumps, you can make the journey smoother.

REACHING EMOTIONAL HEALTH

It is worth noting that the Bible does not deny our emotions, but embraces them. The Psalms are filled with personal testimonies and deep feelings. Here one can discover emotions of rage, skepticism, disappointment, revenge, joy, serenity and peacefulness. And for each of these, there is the affirmation that God is available to help us in our time of need, or to come alongside of us to share our joy.

Unlike people of old, however, we have come a long way in understanding the connections between our feelings and our bodies. We know that untreated depression can lead to physical ailment, or that laughter actually affects the chemicals in our bodies, decreasing our risk of heart disease and stroke. A medical doctor I knew once told me that it takes forty-three muscles to frown, yet only seven facial muscles to smile—clear evidence that we have to work harder to be unhappy and to make others miserable. Yet despite these many evidences—many forthcoming from the medical community—we continue to downplay the need for solid emotional health in the church.

Not long ago, at a clergy gathering, I was struck by how many of my peers were overweight, sallow or sluggish. At that same meeting, the results of a survey were announced, showing that many of the clergy suffered from forms of depression, unresolved anger or apathy. A smaller segment suffered from stresses at home or from ongoing conflicts within the parishes they were serving. The connections, I felt, between the body and the spirit could not have been more telling.

Of course, it is not only clergy who suffer from these emotional struggles, but a good deal of the American populace also. We have become a nation of overeaters, overachievers and undersleepers. We work longer hours, consume more, sleep less and play harder than any previous generation. It is no wonder that our supersized appetites have also led to supersized bodies and egos—and to supersized emotional problems.

A conversation I had some months ago with a gentleman in a hospital lobby is a fitting example of the finely tuned connections between our emotional needs and our physical ailments.

I met this man purely by happenstance as I was sitting with another family in a surgical waiting room. He was positioned next to me, his gaze fixated on the lobby television, and when the family left momentarily to get a bite to eat, he quickly started up a conversation. He introduced himself as Bob, asked for my name and then handed me a business card. "If you're ever in the market for a house," he told me, "give me a call."

"Oh, you're a real estate agent?" I asked.

"Among other things," he stated. He then went on to detail all of the sidelines and businesses he was engaged in, the points of interest—like the four winds of the earth—that fought for his attentions and consumed his days. As he talked, I noted that he was fidgety and nervous. He couldn't sit still.

"Are you waiting to visit someone in intensive care?" I asked.

"My dad's recovering from heart surgery," he told me. Then, as if he were talking to a long lost friend, he quickly summarized his father's life with a few snippets of information. "Dad was never home when I was a kid," he said. "But I haven't held it against him. He was a good provider. He nearly worked himself to death."

I was about to make the observation that Bob was following in his father's footsteps when my new friend countered with the obvious. "Of course, I can't rest, either," he said jokingly. "The moment I sit down, I feel like I should be accomplishing something. I'm always burning the candle at both ends. All of my ex-wives have left me for the same reasons. I don't see my kids very often. So I guess you could say I'm something of a workaholic."

I couldn't help but note the physical condition of this man—who appeared to be ten or fifteen years older than he actually was. His emotional condition—the lifelong attempt to measure up to his father's standard, his inability to connect with his family, his fixation with achievement—had left him physically weak and vulnerable. He was moving down the same road as his father, who was now recovering from a heart attack behind the doors of the intensive care wing.

As I talked to this man, I thought of Jesus's words: "Come unto me all you that labor and are heavy laden, and I will give you rest, for my yoke is easy and my burden is light" (Matt. 11:28–30, my paraphrase from KJV). I scrawled these words on the back of my own business card and gave it to him before he departed.

Somehow, this seemed like the real healing that needed to take place in his life.

THE ILLUSION OF "FEELING" BETTER

Of course, our emotional needs go far beyond just "feeling" better. When emotional healing takes place, it is a work of God, or the helpful work of our family and friends—not something we manufacture on our own or muster up the strength to accomplish through pure willpower. Healing takes place when there is a flow of grace through our lives—from God or through the agency of human intervention and insight. Acceptance and love and laughter have great healing powers—especially when it comes to our emotional health.

I think of one particular trip to Israel as I write this—two moments when I was able to stand on the shores of the two great bodies of water in that region: the Sea of Galilee and the Dead Sea. It is fitting to note that both of these lakes are made of the same water—moisture flowing down from the hills, from the spring rains or from water coursing through the narrow banks of the Jordan River. And yet, these lakes are quite different. The Sea of Galilee is a body of water teeming with life and abundance—a source of fish and a wellspring of sustenance. The Dead Sea, on the other hand, is stagnant—and as its name implies, quite devoid of any life.

What is the difference?

The Sea of Galilee has an outlet. Its waters are released, for its waters flow out to become the Jordan River. The Dead Sea, however, has no outlet. It gives nothing. It only receives—and is, therefore, quite dead indeed.

The same is true of our human condition—especially when it comes to our emotional makeup and the nature of our need. Our emotions must be expressed—they must flow from the center of our being. And if they do, these feelings give life to others, or release us to live more fully. Emotions, however, that are bottled up, emotions that never break free, are like stagnant waters inside us. These emotions—whether they are love or hate, caring or greed—poison us if they are not vented, if they are not offered up in healing and wholesome ways.

Anger kept inside can lead to depression—which is anger unexpressed. Love that goes unexpressed can lead to bitterness—which is love unreciprocated. Joy that is kept in seclusion can lead to apathy—which is frustration. Regardless of our emotions, we are meant to find an outlet for them—creatively if we have to—but an outlet nonetheless.

Consider, for example, the person who does not give his or her whole passions to a job. In time, the work itself will become a labor—just a series of meaningless movements and days without any purpose. And what of the marriages where people do not express their true selves to the other—where intimacy and joy are never really developed, where two people do not become as one? In time, the relationship itself wilts, the passions wane, the communication dries up and the bond eventually breaks.

Surely the same is true of any walk of life—of any facet of life where our emotional center helps us to become what God intends. Without healed emotions—unless we become whole people—we surely wilt and die on the inside.

Trying to feel better about a situation or trying to bring ourselves to feel something that is not real—these are illusions that cannot truly heal us. If we struggle with feelings of perfectionism, the healing may come in time, through circumstances and people and the realization that only God is perfect—and this perfection is enough. Or if we struggle with anger, we are not likely to rid ourselves of this feeling simply by willing it so—especially not immediately. One emotion must replace the other. Anger must give way to understanding or acceptance or a sense of justice fulfilled.

In our culture, we make so many decisions based upon how we "feel." Although our feelings are important, they do not always lead us to make wise decisions. This is another aspect of God's healing grace—the ability to see beyond our emotions.

So often, two people talk about "being in love" or "falling in love" without ever asking the deeper question: Why am I *choosing* to love this person?

The media and books and movies are shot through with images of unrestrained vengeance and revenge—giving us the impression that these are the only ways that we can creatively use our anger to render justice in the world.

And when life becomes difficult, there are many who advocate that it is best to simply "end life" rather than work through the pain to achieve wholeness and understanding.

But each of these realities might help us to see how fragile and unpredictable our feelings truly are. How often have we awakened in the morning feeling on top of the world, only to have one bad experience color the entire day, changing our emotional state? Or perhaps we have gone to bed feeling dejected or lonely, only to awaken feeling refreshed and energized. One day we may be happy. The next day we may be sad. And there is no way of accounting for why or how such feelings come over us. Not logically, at any rate.

The truth is, we are creatures of habit and weak emotion. At the same time, we are also stronger and more resilient than we can possibly imagine. Somewhere in between these two extremes is where we live.

But the wonder of life is also found in all of the feelings that God has created. And because God has created us with such a wide array of emotions, surely God can also heal our broken hearts, our bitterness, our anger. God can help us to express our joy, our love, our awe of the mysteries and majesties of life.

Truly, we are wonderfully made.

And when we are whole people, there is a joyous freedom that permeates our lives. All that has been broken is mended. All that is beautiful is observed. God's healing has come.

3
STUDY GUIDE

T he idea of emotional transformation and healing may be
old news to many people. After all, most people have
come to realize that there are strong connections between
our emotional state and our bodies, between our emotions
and our relationships. In fact, our emotional state can affect
most everything we do. Take a few moments to reflect on
your current emotional state. Silently ask: What am I feeling today? What emotions are driving my life? What unexpressed emotions do I need to release?

- What connections do you see between our emotions and
  our physical well-being?
- What emotions do you most often see expressed in your
  home? At your workplace? In your neighborhood? In
  your church? In our world?
- Where have you experienced an emotional healing in
  your life? How did this healing come about?
- Who are some of the healing people in your life?
- What do you think of the author's suggestion of keeping an affirmation file, or a written prayer, to be used
  during the low points of life? What other ideas do you
  have for emotional health?

Take a few moments to read any or all of the following
biblical passages (or divide them with your group): Matthew
15:32; Matthew 26:37, 39, 50; John 11:35; John 12:7–8.
What emotions is Jesus displaying in each? What do these

passages reveal to us about emotions? What positive expressions of emotion do you discover from these passages?

Prayer: God of all creation, you have made us to feel. We thank you for the ability to share our lives and our loves with others. We are thankful that we have the ability to communicate with, to feel and to know the heart of others. Heal our damaged emotions and stir up those places in our lives where we have walled ourselves off from others, or where unexpressed feelings torment us. Help us to express the highest and the best of ourselves with those we love and with those who threaten us or would do us harm. Through all of life, bring us once again to the fullness of your joy, and give us reason to laugh, to love and to learn. Amen.

CHAPTER 4

Theological Healing: Renewing How We Think About God

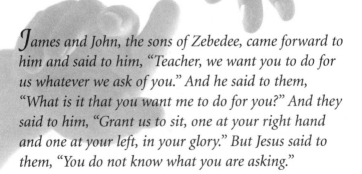

James and John, the sons of Zebedee, came forward to him and said to him, "Teacher, we want you to do for us whatever we ask of you." And he said to them, "What is it that you want me to do for you?" And they said to him, "Grant us to sit, one at your right hand and one at your left, in your glory." But Jesus said to them, "You do not know what you are asking."

—Mark 10:35–38

*N*o doubt, many will look at the title of this chapter and ask: What, exactly, is theological healing? This is a good question, and one that I have pondered as I studied the various forms of healing portrayed in the Bible.

But what I discovered was, much to my delight, there are many instances in the Bible where people are asked to change their minds, or, more specifically, to change the way they think about God or God's work in the world. As Christian people, we are also asked to live our lives in this way—with an open mind, a mind willing to be transformed by the ongoing grace of God. This "change of mind" or "mind change" comes from the Greek word μετανοια which means literally "transformation of the mind or thought," and is an idea that is found throughout the New Testament (as well as the entirety of the scriptures).

In my years as a pastor, I have known many Sunday school classes or small groups that have selected this word as their class name—Metanoia. Hopefully, that is the kind of adventure and undertaking that is ongoing in the group and in their discussions—for I think the concept of "mind transformation" is a vital one, especially as we think of changing the direction of our lives or allowing God to work in new and fresh ways or being open to God's new wonders.

Metanoia represents theological healing: those ways in which God transforms our minds (our thoughts, ideas and ideologies) into a fuller representation of our humanity, into the kind of people we were created to be. It is one of the brightest and highest concepts having to do with our repentance and redemption, and I would like to explore it more fully, for there is no doubt that the transformation of the mind is a form of healing.

Perhaps a few personal insights might help to clarify these matters.

Not long ago I received a summons in the mail asking me to appear for jury duty. I made arrangements, put my pastoral work on hold and drove downtown to perform my civic responsibility. And there I sat—for hours—waiting for my name to be called.

During one of the breaks, however, I found myself gathered in a small circle of men who were casually discussing the news of the day and offering opinions about sports and politics. Eventually the conversation turned to work.

"What do you do for a living?" one fellow asked me.

"I'm a United Methodist pastor," I said.

Immediately the fellow grew pale, almost embarrassingly uncomfortable, and then his face flushed deep red with anger. Suddenly he let loose with a torrent of profanity that peeled a few of the other men away from the circle. "I've had bad experiences with churches," he spouted at one point. "Christians are always professing one thing and doing another. They condemn others, but do the same things themselves. Too many hypocrites."

Honestly, it was not his profanity or his accusations that bothered me the most, but his quick and sudden anger toward anything or anyone representing God. I was initially taken aback, and quite embarrassed myself, but once I recovered I said slowly, "You're right, the church is often full of hypocritical and conflicted people. Pastors see this every day. Often, Christians do profess one thing and live another. There are many who don't live out the faith very well, pastors included. But I think this shows how deeply marred we are and how much we are in need of God's grace."

He softened somewhat, but then added, "I think a lot of Christians are the ones who need to be changed."

I couldn't have agreed with him more. So many of the parables of Jesus were directed at the religious folks of his day—the people who thought they were superior to others or who believed they had a toehold on God's truth and mercy. Jesus even said that the prostitutes and tax collectors would enter the kingdom ahead of the religious folks (that's you and me!). And the biggest accusation leveled against Jesus by the religious leaders was that he "ate and drank with sinners." In other words, they judged Jesus from the company he kept, and believed that "righteous" people had no business associating with "unrighteous" people. The disciples got caught up in this theology, too, and they couldn't seem to bring themselves to accept children, strangers or poor people when they were in the company of Jesus.

How often I have been reminded of these truths by those looking at the church from the "outside"—people who have reminded me that spiritual healing is not only needed by those who are far off from God, but also by those who believe themselves to be spiritually elite or who condemn others for their lack of belief. Perhaps this is even more acute among those who are faithful and devout Christians (yet somehow miss the central meaning of being followers of Jesus).

That fellow in the courthouse could not have been more accurate—at least from the vantage point of his experience—for each of us is in need of change. We have need, somewhere in our thinking, to change an idea or two about God or to transform the way we think about God's work in the world. This may be especially true for people who have grown cold or callused in their faith or who merely go through the motions of religious practice, having a form of religion but no fire in the belly. Others may need to be healed of their apathy or their religious ire—their anger or prejudices, perhaps, toward people of other faiths or creeds. Still others might need healing from religious pride—the belief that they are superior to other people or other Christians. All of these forms of spiritual blindness and elitism add to the misery of the world.

Consider the first group of disciples—those fishermen, young women and tax collectors who followed Jesus from Galilee. They were not above these feelings of elitism either. They had their own ideas about God and about their place and role in the coming kingdom. Mostly, they wanted the highest places of honor.

In one particular episode, the fishermen James and John, the sons of Zebedee, approach Jesus with a request. Although it is not detailed in the text, we can sense that these brothers—like many people today who are trying to do their best for their families—have a great deal of ambition and a strong work ethic.

They come to Jesus asking a favor—a favor that they certainly expect Jesus to grant.

"Give us first and second place in your kingdom," they ask Jesus.

But Jesus counters quickly, and explains that these positions, these prizes, are not his to grant. Then he goes on to offer the disciples a new definition of power. "Whoever wishes to be the greatest," Jesus says, "must become the servant of all" (Mark 10:44).

Indeed, we can imagine that these brothers felt that they had received a good theological thrashing. Their images of power and privilege were skewed. They realized that they did not understand the nature of Jesus himself or his mission and his life. They had to experience a change of mind—not just a change of heart—if they were to understand God's ways.

And that's what theological healing is all about: mind change, mind transformation.

So often in the church, we find a one-dimensional presentation of Jesus. And the emphasis of our faith can become one-dimensional as well, with the focus being laid at the doorstep of a heart change or social transformation, when in fact Jesus asks that we change our minds as well. Mind change, in fact, leads to other forms of transformation and healing.

The apostle Paul spoke eloquently of this change of mind when he wrote to the Romans: "I appeal to you therefore, brothers and sisters, by the mercies of God, to present your bodies as a living sacrifice, holy and acceptable to God, which is your spiritual worship. Do not be conformed to this world, but be transformed by *the renewing of your minds,* so that you *may discern* what is the will of God—what is good and acceptable and perfect" (Rom. 12:1–2, emphasis mine).

There are many instances in the Gospels where Jesus asked people to reconsider, to think more deeply or to change their minds. Sometimes Jesus would challenge preconceived images of God—as he often did when he talked to the Pharisees or with the woman at the well of Samaria (John 4:1–30). Sometimes Jesus is presented as engaging in deep, theological discussion, as we can see when he talked to Nicodemus (John 3:1–21).

So the Gospel is not just a message about a changed heart or a change of direction, but also a changed mind. Often we can see how people's images of God, or their beliefs about God, become destructive rather than healing.

MIND TRANSFORMATION

Consider, for example, the ways in which our belief systems can often support or justify destructive behavior or attitudes. There are many people who consider themselves saintly and dedicated followers of Jesus who support racism or sexism with a theological foundation. They may believe that the Bible teaches that some races are superior and others inferior. And I have met many men who support a subtle brand of sexism based on the belief that God has given them a preordained role of domination and subjugation over women and children. They believe that their role as husband or father, as "head of the house," gives them the right to make all the decisions, administer all of the finances or even control what the rest of the family does. In fact, many can quote certain biblical passages that they believe give them this God-given right to lord their desires over their wives and children.

But these images of God and the Bible do little to transform us with the humble servant mind-set that Jesus talked about (Mark 10:35–45), or the transformed equality that was shared in the early church (Eph. 5:25–33). So often we need to be healed of our misguided thoughts, ideas and hostile notions of power—especially if we have built our lives upon faulty theology or biblical interpretation. We can focus on the periphery of faith rather than living in the center of the Gospel. Clearly, the scriptures make it plain that the goal of the Christian life is that we might be transformed, day by day, into the image and likeness of Jesus, who was pure, loving and humble of heart.

Racism, sexism, elitism, denominationalism and other forms of theological power do nothing to transform our minds into the caring and humble forms of servanthood demonstrated by Jesus. This is why theological transformation can be one of the most powerful forms of healing we can experience. This is also why theological transformation not only changes individuals, but sometimes changes entire groups of people.

During the writing of this book, I was swept up in the unfolding drama of Mother Teresa's beatification in Rome. Beatification, in Roman Catholic tradition and theology, is a lengthy process of study and conversation leading up to an official recognition of sainthood. It is noteworthy that Pope John Paul II sped up this process just for Mother Teresa—a woman who dedicated her life to serving the poorest of the earth's poor, predominantly in Calcutta, India.

I found it interesting to listen to the conversations about her life and to the many thoughts that were shared regarding the "miracles" attributed to her. More fascinating yet, although not everyone agreed that Mother Teresa had worked miracles, few, if any, questioned that she possessed the mind and heart of Jesus. Whether Hindu or Christian, Muslim or Jew—and regardless of religious persuasion—people believe that Mother Teresa lived and healed with her simple philosophy of helping those in need.

Indeed, Mother Teresa's life demonstrates what can happen to us when our minds are transformed from a self-centered mindset, to an other-centered way of living. The need for this type of transformation in our world is undeniable, and we can only imagine how our lives would be different if we could fully and completely submit to God's transforming power.

We spend so much of our days focused on ourselves, our personal wants, desires, dreams and goals that we often believe we don't have time to serve others. When there is a death in the community, we feel that we only have time to send a hastily scrawled sympathy card. Or perhaps a friend goes into the hospital and we feel that we only have time to make a quick phone call—likely from a cell phone as we are driving down the highway. Or perhaps we receive an invitation asking us to help with a youth program, but discover that our days are so filled with our own pursuits we have little time to give to others.

We have all experienced these realities in one form or another.

Unlike children, however, who are constantly "changing their minds," or growing in their knowledge and understanding of the world, we adults often settle into a mind-set—a comfortable approach to thinking about life that does little to engage us in the types of transformations that Jesus spoke about. Perhaps that is why Jesus taught that we must become as children in order to enter the kingdom. Giving our minds, as well as our hearts, over to God is an important step in discipleship and should continue throughout our lives. We are called to be learners—which is what the word "disciple" means.

Allowing God to have more of our mind—our thoughts and desires—is no less important than any other aspect of faith. Like that first ragtag group of disciples, we may need theological healing before we can understand the ways of Jesus and his love.

These insights, however, don't have to be so profound and life altering that we cannot experience this healing in some form every day.

I recall, for example, a conversation I had with a retired woman named Doris many years ago. Doris was one of those people who worked diligently in the church and was often the first to volunteer whenever someone needed a hand. We were working in the food pantry in the church basement, restocking the shelves, when I paid her a compliment, mentioning that she was an inspiration to many people. But she seemed shocked by this—even to the point of being troubled by the compliment itself.

"I guess I'm still trying to live up to my mother's expectations," she said eventually.

"What do you mean?" I asked.

Doris went on to explain how, as a child and teenager, her mother had reared her in an ultrastrict faith—a religion that kept her beaten down, paralyzed with fear and the threat of eternal damnation, and was like a watchful eye judging her every waking move. "I grew up believing that God was out to get me," Doris confided. "God wanted nothing less than perfection from me, and somehow, I always had the feeling that I was failing God, and, consequently, failing everyone around me. When I was a little girl, if I didn't finish my vegetables, my mother would invoke God's dissatisfaction as a means of getting what she wanted. If I brought a new friend home from school, my mother would question the friend about her beliefs until the friend was frightened away by my mother's strict and outspoken brand of Christianity. Even as a teenager, I was not allowed to date, and my mother made it clear that any overture or glance toward the opposite sex was dirty, or even worse, putting me in danger of God's damnation."

"But you're married," I pointed out. "You have such a positive outlook on life now. Something must have happened along the way."

"Well, I went away to college," she said. "That first year away from home, I felt both an immense freedom and a horrendous weight of guilt. On the one hand, I knew that I could never live up to my mother's standards. But on the other hand, I still felt that God was going to strike me down if I fell out of line."

"What changed your mind?" I wanted to know.

"It was a gradual thing," Doris said. "As time went by, I came to believe and to understand that God's grace was sufficient. I simply couldn't live in my mother's faith anymore. And when my mother died a few years later—when I turned twenty-seven—I felt as if I could finally leave behind all of that weight, all of that guilt that my mother had heaped upon me. I don't blame her—I loved her—but that was the biggest step in helping me to change my mind about God. I felt as if I went from being a prisoner with God to being a daughter of God."

Like Doris, I have met many people who have been enslaved by religious belief. Some live their lives in depression—in a constant state of unworthiness and shame. Others suffer from low self-esteem—the feeling that they are unworthy of God's loving affections, but must somehow continually earn their way into God's favor. And others—perhaps like that fellow I met in the courthouse—give up on God and faith altogether as an act of rebellion. They would rather live with no faith—or without religious persuasions, perhaps—rather than live a life filled with burdensome religious rules or straightjacket legalism.

There is no doubt that theological healing comes in many expressions, transforming our minds with the warming and affirming grace of God.

That is why, through the centuries, the church has insisted that God's work in our lives is ongoing. God's grace is not only a justifying grace—all that we need for salvation—but also a sanctifying grace, a renewing and working grace. We are *being saved*. We are going *on to* perfection. We are *on the way* with Jesus. God's work within us is not a one-shot deal. Our faith is a deep and personal relationship—as Jesus taught—much like a father and son, or a mother and daughter, might love, and argue, and grow together.

Centuries ago, the reformer Martin Luther talked about three stages of conversion. He believed that our minds are transformed first. Later, as our faith deepens, our hearts are also changed. Finally, he talked about a stage of redemption that he called, "the conversion of the pocketbook"—where all of our desires and worldly pursuits and possessions are offered up to the work of the kingdom.

How sad it is when Christian people stop growing in their faith or become content simply to sit in a pew or serve on a committee. Instead of seeing life as a rich and rewarding walk with God, so many in the church simply grow apathetic in their pursuit of a deeper spirituality or a deeper learning. They no longer see their relationship with God as a joyous pursuit, but a possession that they have already obtained, satisfied that their ticket is already punched.

As Martin Luther pointed out, the work of the Holy Spirit in our lives is ongoing. Not only is heart transformation needed, but mind transformation and desire transformation also. The Gospel continually challenges us to change our minds! We are called to see the new thing that God is doing. We are called to participate in the new creation that God is unfolding in the world. But without a willingness to change and grow, we so often miss what God is creating.

Like children who must continually change their minds and grow in their understanding of the world around them, we need to be always growing in our perceptions and understandings of God. Of course, we have the scriptures to guide us, and the foundations of faith that serve as continuity with the past. But we must not downplay the role of meaningful conversations with others, personal and communal prayer and waiting for discernment. For these transformations, however, we must use our minds as well as our hearts, for God does not ask us to check our brains at the door when we enter the church. Theological growth doesn't just suddenly dawn upon us, but comes through much struggle—like Jacob wrestling with the angel until the morning light.

This biblical account has significance for us, for it represents a mind change, an identity change. In the story, it was only after much struggle that Jacob realized that he had a new identity (Gen. 32:22–30). He was renamed "Israel," which is a fitting name for all people of faith, for the name "Israel" means "one who wrestles (struggles) with God."

Theological healing—the transformation of the mind—is one of the cornerstones of the Christian faith, and no less a form of God's healing touch.

In our world today, it is easy to see how misguided beliefs about God can prove disastrous—not just for the people who espouse the beliefs, but also for those who must live with the consequences. Perhaps, as never before, we need to be in conversation about God, in dialogue regarding beliefs that can be held in common, and working toward a deeper understanding of what God's peace, justice and joy can look like in an increasingly violent and diverse world. Theological healing is needed. And it will be God's work if, and when, people learn to understand more deeply the transforming power of God's grace.

Not long ago, my congregation was blessed to hear Father Elias Chacour speak on the role of the peacemaker in our world. Dr. Chacour is an Israeli citizen, a Catholic priest, a Palestinian by birth and identity, and a deeply committed servant to the work of peace in the Middle East. Father Chacour, who has been nominated for the Nobel Peace Prize on numerous occasions, has worked at bringing together children and teenagers (and now college students) from differing religious backgrounds to talk about peaceful solutions to the difficult problems facing Palestinians and Israelis. His Israeli schools bring together Jews, Muslims and Christians in an atmosphere of dialogue and reconciliation.

These schools are a beacon of hope in a bleak situation. Here, students of various religious, ethnic and national backgrounds can talk to one another about their hopes and dreams for the future, their doubts and fears and their ideas for making peace a workable reality. No doubt, each of these students is learning how to open the mind to God's peaceful possibilities. A closed mind means relegating themselves to living among the tombs. An open mind, a mind willing to be transformed and enlightened by God's grace, means freedom from the chains of the past.

We could learn much from these young people who are struggling with the realities of death and destruction every day and yet are opening their minds to new ways of thinking about their neighbors. When our minds are transformed and we are able to see through new eyes, our world can become more just, more sane, more hopeful. And one step at a time, the world can change also. But only then.

SEEKING GOD'S HEALING

Of course, seeking God's healing for our battered and bruised minds is not always regarded as a form of God's healing. So often when people think of healing, they are fixated on the physical self—a cure for some malady or disease or illness.

But in the Gospels, and in Paul's Epistles, we can see how the healing work of God goes far beyond the physical self. In fact, sometimes a physical healing cannot take place until a person has opened the mind to the possibilities of God's transforming work.

Consider, for example, a very uplifting passage from Philippians—a letter that the apostle wrote while languishing in prison: "Finally, beloved, whatever is true, whatever is honorable, whatever is just, whatever is pure, whatever is pleasing, whatever is commendable, if there is any excellence and if there is anything worthy of praise, think about these things" (Phil. 4:8).

Amazingly, as one reads this short letter, there are many references to God's transforming work of the mind. Paul wanted to make certain that the church at Philippi did not give itself over to despair, cynicism, nihilism or bitterness (though Paul himself might certainly have had every reason to give *himself* over to such thinking). But his letter is filled with encouragement and consolation, and he asks the church to be of the "same mind" as Christ (2:5) and, where differences exist, that these differences may be sorted out through a transformation of the mind (3:14–15).

Paul recognized that peace and cooperation and working toward harmony were not only gifts of the Spirit, but also a healing work of God. Time and again, wherever there were divisions or disagreements in the early church, Paul asked people to think. He asked them to deepen their understanding of God, to be open to new ideas and to open themselves to the transforming power of God's healing.

We can learn how to see these connections, also.

A story, perhaps, can best illustrate this point.

A famous warrior once visited a monastery and asked to see a monk. "Teach me about heaven and hell," the warrior demanded in a threatening voice.

The monk—a humble and quiet man—sized up the warrior with a glance and then said, "So, you want me to teach you about heaven and hell? Why should I? You are big and offish. You are dirty. You smell. And besides that, you have a rusted sword."

Enraged at the monk's attitude, the warrior immediately drew his sword to smite the monk. But as he was readying to strike, the monk bowed his head and said in a soft voice, "That, my friend, is hell."

Overcome with shame and compassion, the warrior returned his sword to its sheath. After a moment of silence, the monk raised his eyes, looked at the warrior and said softly, "And this, my friend, is heaven."

Often in life, our thoughts can get the best of us. We can convince ourselves to worry when there are no worries. We can bring ourselves to accept any number of ideas that not only harm us, but estrange us from God and from others.

But the true healing of the mind always brings us closer to God's ways. When our minds are well, our bodies and our actions can be well, too.

Of course, the connections between our minds and bodies affect our physical health, also. There is still much to learn about these connections, but even in the medical community, there is wide recognition that there is a balance between mind and body that impacts our health.

Back in the early 1990s, Bill Moyers interviewed an array of doctors, ethicists and professors about the relationship between mind and body. These interviews became the basis for a PBS series entitled, *Healing and the Mind*.

In one of these interviews, Bill Moyers talked to Dr. David Felton, professor of Neurobiology and Anatomy at the University of Rochester School of Medicine. At one juncture, Bill Moyers asked this doctor about these mind/body connections that have a healing effect. "Are you saying that what a patient thinks and feels affects recovery?" asked Moyers.

"It appears so," answered Dr. Felton. "We know . . . there is a constant traffic of information that goes back and forth between the brain and the immune system. And certainly we know that hormones are continuously being produced and released, and neurotransmitters are continually talking to target cells throughout the body."[3]

Although you and I may not be able to understand all of the scientific language and ideology, we can certainly appreciate the knowledge that our thoughts do affect our wellness. How we understand ourselves, and God, and our needs can have an impact upon our health. In essence, our biography can so often become our biology. How we think, and what we think about, can have positive or adverse effects upon our health and wellness.

In fact, most physicians, scientists and religious thinkers would agree that we are just now beginning to tap the foundation of this mind/body connection. That is also why so many medical conversations about healing also include elements of faith and hope. Without a clear mind, a focused and active mind, we can so often languish in despair and hopelessness.

Perhaps the apostle Paul said it best. *Be transformed by the renewing of your mind.*

That's what theological healing is about. When we can see God clearly, and know God's abiding grace, we realize that there is far less in life to fear. When our minds are solid and whole, there are fewer things that harm us, fewer worries that haunt us, fewer relationships that scar us. And nothing, as the apostle Paul wrote to the church at Rome, can separate us from the love of God in Jesus Christ (Rom. 8:35).

4
STUDY GUIDE

R efreshing our minds in God's truth and God's new creation is a profound means of healing. Take a moment to
renew your mind now, allowing God's strength to be a
means of change in your life. After a few moments, consider
the following:

- What do you think the scriptures mean by μετακυοια
  or "mind transformation"?
- How might a change of mind affect our health? Our
  relationships? Our work?
- Can you think of ways in which you have experienced
  God's healing through a change of mind?
- How have you prepared your mind to receive God's new
  blessing or work in your life?
- How do you need to change or grow in your understanding of God? What might help you to do this?
- How is your faith different today than it was five years
  ago? Ten years ago? When you were a child? Why do
  you think this is?
- How did some of the personalities in the Bible change
  their minds about God? What happened after these
  transformations?
- How might our physical well-being and our thoughts be
  tied together?
- Can you think of people who have changed your mind
  about God or God's work? How did this change come
  about?

- How might healing and transformation be associated with learning?
- In what ways might God's healing come through what we know or believe?

Read Romans 12:1–2 and Philippians 4:8. Than ask: What types of mind transformation might be reflected in each of these passages? How might these transformations serve as a means of healing?

Prayer: God of wisdom and insight, we confess that we have much to learn. We are not insightful enough to effect our own redemption or good enough in our actions to reflect what we believe. Like children, we desire to grow in our understanding of you and your ways. Heal our minds where they need to be healed and remove from us any negative thoughts that might hinder our relationship with you or with others. Transform our minds as well as our hearts. Amen.

CHAPTER 5

Social Healing: Transforming Our Sense of Community

He entered Jericho and was passing through it. A man was there named Zacchaeus; he was a chief tax collector and was rich. He was trying to see who Jesus was, but on account of the crowd he could not, because he was short in stature. So he ran ahead and climbed a sycamore tree to see him, because he was going to pass that way. When Jesus came to the place, he looked up and said to him, "Zacchaeus, hurry and come down; for I must stay at your house today." So he hurried down and was happy to welcome him. All who saw it began to grumble and said, "He has gone to be the guest of one who is a sinner." Zacchaeus stood there and said to the Lord, "Look, half of my possessions, Lord, I will give to the poor, and if I have defrauded anyone of anything, I will pay back four times as much." Then Jesus said to him, "Today salvation has come to this house, because he too is a son of Abraham. For the Son of Man came to seek out and to save the lost."

—Luke 19:1–10

One of the greatest misunderstandings about the Christian Gospel is the idea that God's salvation and healing is primarily directed at the individual. This confusion is especially abundant in American churches where individual rights, pursuits and expressions form the foundation upon which American society is built. These individualistic ideas have, naturally, influenced much of our thinking in the church, making it easier for us to miss the larger picture of God's redeeming work.

My hunch is that if we could conduct a survey among average Christians in America, we would discover that it is quite commonplace for folks to believe that God's primary concern is for the individual need, the individual soul, the individual life. The prevailing concept of Christianity, and God's redeeming work, would border on something akin to the notion that each of us relates to God individually—much like independent subcontractors—and therefore we have little spiritual need for anything resembling a family, a congregation or a people. Greater emphasis would be placed on the individual prayer, the individual relationship, the individual need, often at the expense of seeing any connections between the message of the Gospel of Jesus and our relationships with one another.

But a closer reading of the Gospels (and the entirety of the Bible for that matter) reveals a far deeper social dimension to our redemption and healing than we might imagine. Consider, for example, that Abraham and Sarah were called to be spiritual parents of a people—a people who would become as the stars of the sky or the sands of the sea—without number. The prophets, likewise, were rarely sent to individuals. Or when they did speak before the king, or the leaders of their day, they most often spoke in terms of judgment or redemption for the nation whom the king represented. God usually sent the prophets to speak to the people—often critically, but sometimes with great depth of passion, forgiveness and hope. The prophets were not so concerned for the individual that they missed the wider implications of speaking on behalf of the widows, the orphans and the poor.

READER/CUSTOMER CARE SURVEY

We care about your opinions. Please take a moment to fill out this Reader Survey card and mail it back to us.
As a special **"thank you"** we'll send you exciting news about interesting books and a valuable **Gift Certificate.**

Please PRINT using ALL CAPS

First Name _____   MI. _____   Last Name _____

Address _____

City _____   ST _____   Zip _____

Phone # (_____) _____ – _____   Fax # (_____) _____ – _____

Email _____

(1) Gender:
_____ Female   _____ Male

(2) Age:
_____ 12 or under
_____ 13-19
_____ 20-39
_____ 40-59
_____ 60+

(3) Marital Status
_____ Married
_____ Single
_____ Divorced/Widowed

(4) Did you receive this book as a gift?
_____ Yes   _____ No

(6) How did you find out about this book?
Please fill in ONE.
1) _____ Recommendation
2) _____ Store Display
3) _____ Bestseller List
4) _____ Online
5) _____ Advertisement
6) _____ Catalog/Mailing
7) _____ Interview/Review (TV, Radio, Print)

(7) Where do you usually buy books?
Please fill in your top TWO choices.
1) _____ General Bookstore
2) _____ Christian Bookstore
3) _____ Online
4) _____ Book Club/Mail Order
5) _____ Price Club (Costco, Sam's Club, etc.)
6) _____ Retail Store (Target, Wal-Mart, etc.)

(9) What subjects do you enjoy reading about most? Rank only FIVE. Use 1 for your favorite, 2 for second favorite, etc.

	1	2	3	4	5
1) Parenting/Family	○	○	○	○	○
2) Relationships	○	○	○	○	○
3) Recovery/Addictions	○	○	○	○	○
4) Health/Nutrition	○	○	○	○	○
5) Christian Living	○	○	○	○	○
6) Inspiration	○	○	○	○	○
7) Business Self-Help	○	○	○	○	○
8) Teen Issues	○	○	○	○	○
9) Sports	○	○	○	○	○

(14) What attracts you most to a book?
(Please rank 1-4 in order of preference.)

	1	2	3	4
1) Title	○	○	○	○
2) Cover Design	○	○	○	○
3) Author	○	○	○	○
4) Content	○	○	○	○

TAPE IN MIDDLE; DO NOT STAPLE

BUSINESS REPLY MAIL
FIRST-CLASS MAIL PERMIT NO 45 DEERFIELD BEACH, FL

POSTAGE WILL BE PAID BY ADDRESSEE

FAITH COMMUNICATIONS
3201 SW 15TH STREET
DEERFIELD BEACH FL 33442-9875

FOLD HERE

Which Faith Communications book are
you currently reading?

Comments:

Their message swept across the land and was not chiefly directed at the individual life.

Likewise, we cannot miss the fact that Jesus came to establish a movement that was later called "the church." And while it is also true that Jesus called individuals to be a part of this movement, he did not intend for the work of the kingdom to be individualistic. It should be noted, for example, that Jesus not only called a "group" of followers, but he always sent the disciples out in pairs or in groups when there was kingdom work to be accomplished. Likewise, as Jesus traveled about the regions of Galilee and Judea, he was always accompanied by this group of followers or learners (disciples), and when Jesus touched individuals or healed them, he almost always did so within the context of some social injustice or some larger need beyond the individual.

To illustrate this point, let's take a quick look at three Gospel stories where God's healing touch or presence is seemingly offered solely to the individual. Although it may seem from a quick reading that each of these accounts is individualistic in nature, in fact, all of them contain far greater social implications for healing and wholeness than we might imagine.

The Man by the Pool

Our first story is found in John 5:2–15. Here we encounter a man who has lived for thirty-eight years by the pool of Bethsaida—a place where many invalids who are blind, lame or paralyzed have congregated in the hope of being healed of their infirmities. Jesus enters the area and heals the man with the simple instruction to "rise, take up your mat, and walk."

But there are three elements of this story that can be missed entirely—all of them bearing important social weight—that make this man's healing not just an individual event, but a testimony to our need for community and connectedness. Consider, first of all, that this man has been clearly visible to the community around him. And he has been languishing by the pool within reach of many people for thirty-eight years. When Jesus asks the man if he wants to be healed, the man quickly points out that no one has stopped to help him. Not a single helpful soul in nearly four decades!

Although the man clearly is using this fact an as excuse, we can see that the greater weight lay with the community around him. Where are the helpful people? Where are the willing hands? Where are the people who are eager to assist in this man's healing and redemption?

They can be found nowhere!

Second, we cannot overlook the fact that Jesus heals this man on the Sabbath. (Note how often Jesus heals on the Sabbath in other stories!) To do anything on the Sabbath was an act of community and covenant. And so we can see that in this man's healing, Jesus is also making a statement: this man is being restored to the religious community from which he has been ostracized and left unable to participate. This was true of all who had physical impairments in first-century Judea. An illness automatically excluded a person from the community's prayers, as well as from the sacrifices, offerings, and sustenance received from the scriptures and acts of worship. The religious community could have healed this man (this is made plain in the story), but people chose to exclude the man on account of his illness (and for religious reasons, I might add).

Finally, we see that the man's initial witness to his healing is social in nature. He tells his story to others—and so becomes a witness to God's greatness. He cannot keep this marvel to himself. His healing is not individualistic—not "a personal and private matter" (as many Americans will often insist if asked about their faith)—but social and interpersonal.

The healing of the man by the pool of Bethsaida offers a rich social tapestry for us to look upon—and compels us to ask some very penetrating questions about ourselves and our time. Are we passing by people in the church or on our streets or refusing to look upon their need when we could easily offer them healing through a kind word or a helping hand? Is all healing really so physical in nature—or are there other elements of healing that come into play when a person discovers love, acceptance and the support of a caring community? Could we do these works of Jesus today?

Blind Bartimaeus

Let's turn our attention now to a second account, found in Mark 10:46–52. Here Jesus heals a blind man named Bartimaeus—one of the few people mentioned in the Gospels by name. Again, from the outset, this may seem like an open-and-shut case of one man receiving one healing from one Jesus of Nazereth. But let's look more closely.

In this story, Jesus and his followers are leaving Jericho when they encounter a blind man sitting beside the road. (Maybe he is holding up a sign—WILL WORK FOR FOOD.) When Bartimaeus realizes that Jesus is passing by, he begins to shout, "Have mercy on me!" Quickly, others move in and sternly order him to hush up! But he cries out all the more. Finally, Jesus calls the man, the crowd responds by taking the man to Jesus, and after some preliminary questions, Jesus gives Bartimaeus his sight.

As with the healing of the man by the pool of Bethsaida, this story offers us some deeper social truths that we can easily miss.

One will note, for example, that the crowd mentality plays a large role in this story. There are many people around who are eager to keep the blind man quiet. After all, he has been blind his entire life (he has never known sight), and he seems to be something of an embarrassment to the people in that region. Perhaps this healing story quickens our awareness of the role we might play in discouraging someone. Perhaps, like the people in Jericho, we can often think that people deserve what they get, or that we play no role in encouraging someone to find an avenue of hope. The social mentality here is initially one of fatalism and discouragement—"just keep quiet, Bartimaeus, and don't rock the boat!"

We can also observe in this account that the outcome of the healing (actually even *before* the healing) was socially transforming. When Jesus calls, others respond with their assistance. They offer Bartimaeus a helping hand; they tell him to take heart. And in the end, Bartimaeus becomes one of the followers of Jesus—he becomes part of a *community*—a reality, perhaps, that he has never before experienced in his life.

Before Jesus came along, Bartimaeus was no doubt a lonely man. He, like the man by the pool of Bethsaida, was not allowed access to the religious life of the people. And now he was with Jesus himself!

Bartimaeus did not experience only a physical healing. His healing was socially transforming. And although it is not mentioned in the text, we can assume that many people returned to Jericho with a newfound hope and encouragement as well.

This story contains so many implications for our time.

Today, you and I live in a fast-paced and lonely culture where we pass by people in need almost every day. We have all seen the WILL WORK FOR FOOD signs, have read about the number of children who are hungry and know of people in need who go to our schools, shop in our supermarkets and attend our churches. It is easy to fall into a pattern of cynicism and discouragement, where (if even only secretly) we wish that we did not have to deal with the embarrassment of these lives around us, or we attempt to explain away these forms of suffering by throwing the weight of the situation back on the individual who is in need. (If only they would get a job or clean themselves up or get some help.)

But encouraging words can often bring people to places they never dreamed. God knows each of us by name, and calls to us by name, and one of the greatest joys of the Gospel is when we get to help each other experience God's touch. Bartimaeus could not have found Jesus without the crowd, and his witness would have been little or nothing if Jesus had healed him in some solitary act along the outskirts of town.

This story is a witness to the transforming power of our own words—and our helpfulness—when we are willing to offer ourselves to others. The healing of Bartimaeus changed not one life, but many. And the same can happen to us.

The Samaritan Woman by the Well

Our final illustration can be found in John 4:5–40—one of the most well-known accounts in the Gospels. Here Jesus travels with his disciples into the region of Samaria—an area through which most Jews of the day would not travel, but would walk around. There, while sitting beside Jacob's well, Jesus encounters a woman who engages him in a most interesting conversation. Through the course of this conversation we learn that the woman is religious, that she can express her faith well and that she also lives something of a sordid life—with numerous husbands and a current live-in boyfriend.

Over the years as I have heard sermons preached from this text, the most common point of fixation seems to be upon the sexual innuendo found in the text—and it is certainly there. But this account is also one of the most socially acute texts to be found anywhere in the Bible, and that, along with the healing moment, is often overlooked.

Let's take a deeper look.

As most Bible students know, this story is significant because it takes place in Samaria, among a people who were despised by the Jews living in the surrounding regions of Galilee and Judea. This setting carries great weight, for we see Jesus entering into a despised and rejected world to live among an outcast population. *Anything* that happens here—especially when a Galilean Jew speaks to a Samaritan—has great social implication.

Notice that Jesus breaks several social taboos of the time—and all of them at once! He drinks from a Samaritan well (which might have made Jesus ritually unclean, in the mind-set of the time). He converses with a woman in a private setting (breaking another taboo). And he even delves into her personal life (most certainly a guarded subject then as it is today).

Jesus discovers that, although the woman has a deeply refined spirituality, her personal life is a mess. And by the time he finishes speaking to her, she is so flustered and excited that she leaves her water jar behind (she forgot why she came to the well) and goes back into the village to tell others about Jesus. Likewise, the disciples are flustered when they return and discover Jesus talking to this woman (they are aghast). And by the end of the story, many people in the village believe in Jesus and even ask him to stay with them. And Jesus does stay—for two days, sleeping overnight in their homes and eating their food— two more big taboos that break down more social barriers than we can even imagine.

But what does this story have to say to us today? What are the implications for social healing in our time?

For one, I've always found a richness in this text that speaks directly to our idea of individual privacy—the idea that our personal lives are no one else's business, not even God's. The fact that this woman had a deep spirituality, but a distressed personal life, is worth noting. The Samaritan woman could serve as a poster child for our time—in an age where the outward appearance does not always match up with the inner reality. We can read almost every day about the disparities that exist between a person's faith profession and their inner demons. In our time, we have witnessed the rise of "Disneyland faith"—where millions of dollars are received over the airwaves and religious personalities live lavish lifestyles—all at the expense of the poor and the needy (who are quite willing to send in money because they *are* needy and the television personalities possess the lifestyle and offer the promises that desperate people desire to snatch). We have read stories of pedophile priests, abusive youth ministries and drug addiction among those who serve in Christ's name. And on a far more personal level, we can often see the deficiencies and sins in those who preach, those who teach or those who are considered pillars of the church. Go deeper yet and we can see these disparities within ourselves.

Of course, all of these realities point in the direction of a deeper truth. We have a need to live a life that is whole, a life of integrity—not a life that is faithful on Sunday and another way the other six days of the week. And still deeper yet, we have a need for God to recreate us, to make us whole. We have a need for God to know us intimately, and to heal us of the sins and infirmities that separate us from one another.

These truths have deep social connections.

As in the story of the woman of Samaria, we can see that being a disciple of Jesus requires that we change our outlook and our ways. Those first disciples had to grow in their thinking when they passed through Samaria; they had to be willing to accept people who, before, they may have considered unacceptable.

I think Jesus took that first band of disciples through Samaria in order to demonstrate that one couldn't have prejudice and follow him at the same time. A disciple has to be willing to interact with those who are different, who may look, act or believe differently. A disciple can't despise another person—a person who is also created in the image of God.

Perhaps, as the old adage states, we learn that a friend is a stranger we have yet to meet. When these social barriers are broken down, the kingdom of God is seen more fully and completely.

SOCIAL CONNECTIONS AND THE CHURCH

We also see the social dimensions of the healing Gospel whenever we read the apostle Paul's letters (Epistles). It is noteworthy that nearly all of Paul's letters were written to churches, to groups of people. The implications of the Gospel that Paul addresses are predominantly social in nature.

When he writes to the church at Corinth, for example, he ends up offering them a new image of the church: not just a collection of individuals, but a body—much like the human body—that functions in much the same manner as the coordination of hand and eye. A body is incomplete unless all members are working together. All of these images are socially profound and form the basis of one of the most common images of the community we call the church (1 Cor. 12).

Likewise, those letters written to individuals—such as Philemon—contain radical social implications and commentary, such as Paul's request that Philemon release Onesimus from his bond of slavery (Philem. 1:13–16), a request that may have fallen on deaf ears. Or in the letter of 1 Timothy, the apostle addresses the role of various leaders in the church and offers his commentary on the social implications of a leader's personal life (1 Tim. 3:1–13). Even the individual books are not private, and the weight these Epistles carry in helping us to see the social dimensions of God's healing touch is tremendous.

On a personal level, I have experienced these forms of social healing many times. Before and following my wife's breast cancer surgery, we experienced the loving touch of community, the prayers and support of others—which became God's healing touch for us. During the weeks leading up to the surgery, we received many cards and letters of support—some from people we had not seen in years—telling us that they were praying for us and were not going to forget us. Following the operation, many people brought food by the house or volunteered to keep the children or run errands. Our family also surrounded us with so much love, and we never lacked for help or support.

I have no doubt that these connections with others—their prayers and their presence—had a healing impact upon my wife's body. There was no way we could simply point to the surgery itself as a healing factor (though it was a large one!)—but we became aware of other sources of healing and strength that flowed into our lives through other people.

Likewise, I have known many people who have experienced healing after they have discovered meaningful connection with others. Although not all of these healings came through the community of the church, the principles and power of social healing are the same.

Consider, for example, the number of people who have been healed of alcoholism through the social connections of Alcoholics Anonymous. There are also many who have found healing after the death of a spouse because their friends and neighbors showed concern. Other people have found healing through exploring the arts (sharing their expressions with others), or expressing their pain in support groups or therapy sessions with like-minded people.

I have also known teenagers who have emerged from drug addiction with a new zest for life only after they were confronted by the loving concern of family and friends. After my wife's cancer, I noted how many women had discovered healing community in cancer support groups—where Christian, Jewish and Muslim women all shared their experiences. And I could go on, for the communities in which we live our lives and find healing are many.

I think this is why Jesus always touched people in a social context. It is why he called a group of followers to become leaders and supportive helpers. Jesus wanted to make clear that the context of healing is always social in nature—not an individual pursuit—and that what we do for others in his name has great weight and significance.

Long ago, in the first centuries of the church, community was far more important than we can imagine today. During the days of religious persecution, no one could survive by being an island—an individual believer. There were underground support networks, and the healing ministry of the church was linked from one family to another, often through signs such as the fish or the cross. In time, as the church flourished and became accepted, the Lenten season leading up to Easter was a time when people who had fallen away from the church, or who had committed significant sins, were restored to the fellowship. This restoration was often accompanied by the laying on of hands (carrying healing import) or via confession before the body of believers. There was no such thing as an individual Christian separate from the community.

These realities bring us full circle to our time—where we often attempt to live our faith in the privacy of our hearts or our homes or as tiny enclaves of independent believers. Our idea of the church and of the Christian faith is markedly different from the early centuries of the church and from the social context of the Gospels, where redemption and wholeness and healing were regarded as socially altering movements of God. So often, we turn inward to find God's healing. But the touch of Jesus comes to us through the healing body of the church (imperfect as it is), as we represent the very hands, feet and spirit of Jesus.

Ours is an incarnational faith. And as such, we recognize that God uses human hands—even today—to accomplish the work of the kingdom and to heal those who are broken in body or in spirit. God can use us to heal the world's brokenness, if we are willing.

I think of these things whenever I consider the work that Jesus has given us to accomplish. In Luke 9:1–6, Jesus first gave authority to his people to go into the tiny villages and hamlets of the beautiful region of Galilee, asking them to, among other things, "cure diseases." And so they went. The Gospel says that they traveled into the villages, bringing good news and curing diseases everywhere.

Is our mission any less compelling today? Isn't this an age that needs to hear good news—life-changing, world-changing news? And are there not still many diseases to be cured? Diseases of the mind, of the body and of the human heart?

In fact, we may find ourselves in the most precarious time in human history, when hatreds run so deep that people are willing to blow themselves to bits as a way of destroying the lives of innocent men, women and children at the same time. In a world such as this, don't our hearts need to be healed first? And then, once we have experienced God's healing, doesn't God's love compel us to try to be healers and peacemakers in a world gone mad?

There is nothing individualistic about these realities.

If we are to survive, if we are to experience a better world, we must strive together. There must be movements sweeping over our world other than the movements of hatred. There must be forms of healing being offered other than resources of gauze, bandages and medicine.

We need God's Band-Aid for the soul.

You and I have this wonderful opportunity (and each day is an opportunity!) to help transform God's world into wholeness and peace. We, like the prophets of old, can proclaim justice and mercy to a people lost or forgotten; we can work for peace and healing before the darkness swallows us.

We must not forget the final vision that is before us, where the nations are healed (Rev. 22:2) and the light of God overcomes all of our human animosities and atrocities. Our healing and redemption is never complete until we can share it with others.

This is the Gospel. This is the everlasting joy.

5
STUDY GUIDE

T his chapter explores the social dimensions of healing
and the ways in which we touch and change each other.
We are called to be healers and helpers, and there are
many ways we are blessed by others. People who are lonely,
ostracized or afraid often live outside of meaningful community, but can be changed by a kind word or a willing
hand. Reflect on these truths in your own life, then move to
the following questions:

- How is social healing reflected in the Bible?
- What are the implications for the need of social healing
  in our time?
- Is it possible for us to affect another person's healing? How?
- How might community change a person's health and
  outlook on life?
- What types of illnesses might be dramatically affected
  by loving people?
- What types of community have you found meaningful
  in your life?
- What groups of people provide you with support and
  healing when you need it?
- Where do you lack community in your life?
- What do you need most from the church? From your
  family? From your friends?
- What kindnesses might you expend to someone who is
  hurting or suffering? How might your efforts be a healing touch to that person?

Read Acts 2:43–47 and Acts 6:1–6. Then ask: What types of healing and helpfulness are talked about here? What are the connections between these healings and the community that is being formed? What does community have to tell us about the importance of God's work in the world today? How is unity a witness to God's healing touch? What happens when individualism dominates our lives?

Prayer: God, you call us to unity and to serve each other. Just as the body is incomplete without a hand or a leg, we are incomplete without each other. Help us not to neglect the strength of caring community and our place in it. We are not called to be individuals of faith, but a faithful community. Heal us, and help us to be healers of others. Amen.

CHAPTER 6

Bodily Healing:
Recovering from Physical Affliction

He took our infirmities and bore our diseases.

—Matthew 8:17

Are any among you sick? They should call for the elders of the church and have them pray over them, anointing them with oil in the name of the Lord. The prayer of faith will save the sick, and the Lord will raise them up; and anyone who has committed sins will be forgiven. Therefore confess your sins to one another, and pray for one another, so that you may be healed.

—James 5:13–16

*N*ewsweek once ran a feature article about the connections between faith and physical healing. While there was nothing unique about this particular article (just another among thousands written on this topic over the past decades), the feature did bring to light the cooperative efforts of science and faith—particularly as related to the medical treatment of the individual.[4]

Although the scientific evidences for the connections between faith and physical healing are still sketchy at best, there is much solid research suggesting a strong link between the practice of faith and wellness (of body, mind and attitude). People of faith, it has been discovered, tend to live longer, healthier and more upbeat lives, in general, than do people who do not practice a faith. Of course, there may be many reasons for this—including lifestyle choices, deeper and more plentiful relationships, less worry, less stress and a more positive outlook on life. People who belong to organized religions also tend to have more friends, and friendship has been shown to be a factor in length of life. Religious people also tend to have fewer vices, such as smoking, excessive drinking, drug addictions and gambling. But regardless of the factors, most in the medical community do recognize this strong connection between faith and physical well-being.

Naturally, when it comes to scientific evidence, we must guard ourselves from making hasty associations between the validity of all of these connections, but it is worth noting that most of the major medical schools now offer courses in "Spirituality and Health," or similarly titled classes. There is a growing awareness in the medical community that medicine should treat the whole person—not just the body—and that all patients are unique in their individual beliefs, hopes, dreams and attitudes (all of which can play a vital role in the healing process). No doubt, we are just now beginning to tap the connections between science and spirituality.

I mention these things at the beginning of this chapter because, for many people, any discussion of bodily healing can easily fall into one of two camps:

- The idea that all physical healing is achieved purely through scientific means and practices;
- Or the idea that faith in God is all that is required for one to be healed of any disease or malady.

One of the reasons why I chose to place this chapter further along in this book centers on the difficulties posed by these two extremes. I first wanted to establish clarity with regard to the breadth and types of healing we can experience. And then I hoped to make clear that when we are engaged in any discussion of healing, we are never just talking about a body comprised of organs and tissues. We are discussing human beings, in all of their complexity and needs.

Hopefully we can see that healing has many dimensions beyond the physical, and so we should reject those ideas that focus on healing solely as "cure," or as simply a matter of "faith." Likewise, we cannot approach healing from a purely scientific point of view (or from a purely religious point of view, for that matter), for clearly we are dealing with matters of the human heart, mind and creativity—and all of these intricacies and realities point us to a deeper source of life, health and giftedness than exists purely within the current body of human knowledge and practice. And although there is sometimes a tension between those who believe that medicine alone holds the keys to health and those who believe that faith in God makes all things well, there is growing evidence to suggest that there is room for cooperation and mutual understanding between these historically estranged bedfellows.

After all, who better to understand a human sickness than a doctor—a person with knowledge of the human body who has studied and grown and practiced the art of medicine? And who is more qualified to speak of the spiritual complexities of disease and illness than the traditions and experiences embodied in religious communities who have suffered and loved and struggled and died alongside the sick for centuries?

I believe that we can never fully understand the richness and potential of bodily healing until we learn to appreciate and tap into both sides of this equation. Medicine needs the faith community. And faith needs medicine.

A quick glance at one Gospel account may help us to appreciate these connections more fully. In John 9:1–34, we find a lengthy account of a blind man's healing. On the surface, this healing may seem entirely metaphysical, but a closer look will reveal that the blind man's healing also had a medical dimension (at least, a medical dimension that can be associated with the knowledge of the time).

The account goes like this: Jesus and the disciples are walking along when they see a man who has been blind from birth. The disciples ask Jesus, "Who sinned, this man or his parents, that he was born in this condition?" Jesus doesn't buy into the theology of punishment and tells his followers that sin has nothing to do with the man's condition. "God's glory will be revealed in this man," Jesus tells them.

Suddenly, Jesus kneels on the dusty road, spits into the soil and makes mud (a crude ointment) that he spreads over the man's eyes. He then tells the man to go and wash his eyes in the pool of Siloam (see John 9:6–7)—a pool (perhaps a mineral spring?) often associated with healing in first-century Judea. When the man returns to Jesus, he can see.

Of course, this is a fascinating story in many ways, but for our purposes, it reveals an element of healing that we do not often attribute to Jesus: that of using homemade ointment and soothing water to effect a blind man's sight. This account demonstrates that we cannot discount medicine or faith in a person's healing, for both are evident at one and the same time, even in the healing ministry of Jesus.

No doubt, there is a spiritual dimension to healing. But the practice of medicine may often be the means through which an individual receives the healing touch.

If the previous chapters have revealed anything, I hope that they have shown the connections between these two realities, not only within the context of the Christian faith, but for those who may have a different faith or no faith at all. There is a tendency on the part of many well-meaning people to turn God into a machine at precisely this point: in the idea that God responds to our demands and prayers because God *must respond*. But, of course, human beings do not control God. God—and God's healing touch—is not a commodity that *we control*, as if we were in charge of the universe. Faith in God is, in large part, trusting in the mystery of God's presence and grace. Faith is offering our lives up to God's will—not asking God to conform to our will or what we want.

We also see this truth reflected in the ministry of Jesus in a number of ways. In Mark 2:1–12 we find an account of a man who was brought to Jesus on a mat and lowered through the roof by four friends. What is remarkable about this story is that there is no mention of the man himself having faith. We do not even know if he was a willing participant in his transportation. Only the faith of his friends is mentioned (2:5) and Jesus says nothing at all about the man's physical illness. The man is "cured" of his affliction only after he receives forgiveness (which would seem to indicate that Jesus recognized that the man's affliction was not physical in nature).

The interesting component of this story is that Jesus heals the man (and forgives him) long before he requests it. And when the man does rise and walk, he doesn't say a word, but hastens quickly from the scene, seemingly embarrassed by his unexpected wholeness.

Another fascinating account is Luke 5:12–16. Here Jesus heals a leper. And soon afterward, large crowds gather to hear Jesus and to be cured of their diseases. Jesus, however, doesn't give them what they desire. He withdraws to a deserted place and prays.

The purpose of this story? Perhaps to demonstrate (as if we needed to be reminded of this reality) that not all people receive a physical healing. Jesus did not (could not) meet every need. And likewise, not everyone who asks God for a cure receives one.

Living by faith, we know that we cannot negotiate a healing as if we are buying a used car or making a real estate deal. Nevertheless, one prevalent view that continues to persist in the church is the idea that those who have faith get healed, and those who don't have "enough" faith, or who don't believe, or who don't ask for healing in the proper way or with the correct words, languish and die.

Life itself, however, is our greatest teacher—and life reveals that a theology built upon this foundation (as Job and his well-meaning friends discovered of old) is inaccurate, incomplete and brutal. The "amount" of faith we possess, or "how" we pray or how loudly we make our petitions is not the foundation of God's grace. Grace is a gift.

What we should note about most of the healing accounts of the Bible is this: that the human response to healing is usually one of inexplicable gratitude and thanksgiving. Because bodily healing *is* so miraculous, whether we receive it through chemotherapy, prayer, surgery or some unexpected touch of God, our natural response (even if we don't practice a faith) is one of thanksgiving! We may not be able to explain our healing to someone else (sometimes not even medically) but that doesn't take away from our sense of awe and gratitude—toward God, toward the doctors and toward all who had a hand in our physical restoration. When we are made well, we naturally want to tell others about it and allow them to share this joy with us.

Although not all receive a cure, this does not diminish our human need to rejoice when something wonderful happens to us. Being healed doesn't mean that we are better than someone who languishes and dies (or are more faithful or "right" with God). It just means that we have received a gift—a gift that, by its very nature, calls us to help those who are struggling or hurting or dying.

This is precisely the miracle of grace, and there is, as Jesus taught, an underlying grace of God that pervades all of life and provides the very foundation for life itself. As Jesus said, "God makes the sun shine upon the evil and the good, and sends rain to the righteous and the unrighteous" (Matt. 5:45).

And so we can see (from the scriptures and from experience) that God's grace, which includes healing, extends to many in ways we can scarcely comprehend and is not bound by our conventions or ideas about who is worthy or ready or even willing to receive this grace. In other words, there is a mystery to God's healing touch, and God will do what God desires to do (which is always to do good).

Faith, however, is important at precisely this point. Faith is the awareness of God's presence, God's touch and God's mercy. Faith is the avenue through which God becomes personal and real to us. Faith is trust in God. And when we learn to trust God, there are so many ways that God's healing touch can transform and empower us.

This is the foundation upon which this discussion of bodily healing is based, and I believe it is quite biblical, experiential and sound. When it comes to healing, there is something of a mystery within both realms—that of medicine and that of faith—that we cannot completely grasp or explain. Doctors know this as well as theologians.

Through the years, I have heard many doctors take note of the mysteries of certain procedures or experiments. Perhaps a medication or procedure is tried. One person may recover. Another may die. What is to account for these outcomes? Surely, even medicine itself contains a complexity, and the practice of medicine is certainly something of an art form that cannot be fully contained in the word "science." Some doctors have greater knowledge and expertise. Others less so. Some physicians have a good bedside manner. Others have interpersonal skills that are lacking. Some doctors will laugh with patients. Others will scarcely crack a smile.

Are we so far off to assume that these personal skills, forms of practice and shaping attitudes, whether refined or crude, do not have (at the very least) some negative influence or positive healing effect, as the case may be? Certainly, some doctors—like other personalities we might know—are natural healers. Their touch or their concerned conversation rubs off on other people in a positive and healing manner.

A quick glance at the other side of faith might reveal similar truths. Are we to assume, for example, that the patient who believes her illness is a punishment from an angry God will heal in the same fashion as the patient who believes she is drawing strength from God's helping presence and abiding love? Will someone who is ill find peace *through* faith, or be haunted and tormented *by that* faith? These are large questions, carrying theological, psychological and medical weight. Surely our religious persuasions and ideas (whether helpful or hurtful) have at least a marginal bearing on our physical healing and recovery—don't they?

No doubt, there is still much to learn, but a couple of personal stories might help to illustrate these points.

HEALING AND WHOLENESS

Some years ago, while serving as a volunteer chaplain in a community hospital, I was called upon to visit a young man who had been badly injured in a drive-by shooting. The doctors were telling him that he faced the prospect of being paralyzed from the waist down. When I entered the room to talk, I discovered that he was troubled. But then, I thought, why shouldn't he be? I wouldn't want to face the prospect of living with paralysis either.

However, our conversation soon revealed some deeper concerns. This fellow was struggling with many spiritual questions, some of them having to do with the selling and dealing of illegal drugs; he was estranged from his friends, and he harbored many regrets about the course he had chosen for his life. In short, he wanted to know if forgiveness was possible, and he was particularly grieved by the heartache he had caused his mother. "What would you say to the people you have wronged?" I asked him at one point.

"I want to tell them I'm sorry," he said.

"Do you think you could do that?"

"How can I?" he asked. "God's put me in this bed. I'll never walk again."

His choice of words was fascinating, and we spent time talking about the meaning of forgiveness—both our ability to receive God's forgiveness, and our need to make amends or restitution, wherever and whenever possible, as a means of demonstrating our desire to change and embrace a new life. Then we prayed together—a simple prayer of faith, repentance and forgiveness. We also prayed for his healing.

Some days passed, and the next time I visited this young man, he seemed to be in better spirits. He was working hard at his physical therapy and was actually showing signs of movement in his legs. The doctors were astounded at his progress.

A few weeks later, he was walking with a cane. And months later, he was walking without assistance, though with a noticeable limp.

Looking back on this young man's experience—and the initial prognosis he had received regarding the paralysis—I have to believe that God's healing touch was somewhere in the mix. Like so many stories we find in the Gospels, here was a fellow whose sins and mistakes seemed to be closely tied to his injuries. The healing that this young man received—though not a complete "cure"—was much like those in the Gospel accounts where Jesus forgives the sins of a person and then offers the word of healing and restoration.

We cannot overlook these connections, for they point us in the direction of what it means to be whole. A sick person is not a whole person. And neither is a person who is carrying the weight of sin, regret or broken relationships. The willingness to receive

God's forgiveness is often closely tied to our physical, and certainly our spiritual, well-being.

Sometimes, however, physical illness or denial serves to heighten our awareness of God and the realities beyond the senses. There is a long history in most religious traditions regarding this truth, and we can see nuances of it in those traditions where fasting or physical hardships are willingly assumed, or where people remove themselves from the trappings and distractions of worldly comforts and willingly deprive themselves of outside stimulation.

I have seen this same phenomenon in many people suffering from terminal illnesses.

Linda was one such example. In her late sixties, she had been diagnosed with an advanced stage of lung cancer and was told that she had but a few months to live. At first, Linda struggled with this news (as we all would); she prayed for healing and asked for the prayers of others.

As the weeks progressed, however, and as the disease spread more rapidly through her body, she found herself entering into an unexplainable peace. Although she was weakening daily, her positive attitude and spirit seemed piqued at a constant high. Her illness was a doorway through which she entered into a closer relationship with God.

Once, during one of my visits, I was astounded to hear Linda speak of her healing. From where I was sitting, Linda did not appear to be healed (for she was dying). But from her perspective, God had touched her body and had given her some very valuable time in which to set her house in order, to speak to her family and friends, and to move into a deeper level of the spirit.

Amazingly, although Linda was supposed to live but a few weeks, she lived on for some months—not always in a state of pain or listlessness—and it was only during the final days of her life that she was unable to communicate with others. My experience with Linda taught me a valuable lesson. Although I was unable to see Linda as a healed person (I was looking at cure only) that is precisely how she viewed herself. Who was I to say that she was not healed?

Again, we might hearken back to Bill Moyers's PBS series in the early 1990s entitled *Healing and the Mind.* The premise behind this series was the idea that modern-day science and research has continued to unravel the mysteries of the mind/body connection, leading us back to what ancient philosophers and physicians once believed: that thoughts and feelings do influence our health and can also be a powerful force in our healing.

One of the people interviewed for this series was Rachel Naomi Remen, a medical doctor who founded and directs the Institute for the Study of Health and Illness at Commonweal. Dr. Remen—who is a practicing Jew and a marvelous writer as well as serving as a teacher at some of the most renowned and well-respected medical schools in the country—had much to say about the mind/body relationship and how our thoughts affect our healing and wholeness. Her books, much like Rabbi Harold Kushner's bestselling *When Bad Things Happen to Good People,* have helped to comfort many people and offer God's healing presence in times of need or questioning.

At one point in the interview, Dr. Remen had this observation about the human role in healing: "You know," she said, "every one of us is wounded, and every one of us has healing power. I heal you, and you heal me. That's how it goes in life. Several times a day we may switch those positions. It's not about expertise; it's about something much more natural. We're all wounded healers."[5]

A few decades ago, Henri Nouwen, theologian, priest and writer, penned a book entitled *The Wounded Healer*—a book that reflected on the healing role of the pastor and priest in the modern world and the ways in which God's grace makes all healing possible. His little book sent up a signal in the church and helped us—pastors in particular—to see how God's grace is channeled through human frailties and weaknesses. Like Dr. Remen, Nouwen believed that there is an incarnational element to our lives where God's strength and healing are manifest through the work of our hands or a kind, sympathetic touch.[6] Or, as Jesus taught, we are endowed by the Holy Spirit with gifts sent by God—and some of these gifts are gifts of healing and restoration.

There is no doubt that miraculous healing continues to occur today, but the manifestations of these healings may be far too commonplace for us to notice. Consider, for example, the number of people we know who have recovered from heart disease, cancer, kidney failure or some traumatic stress upon the body, such as a car accident or blow to the head. Had many of these people suffered from these illnesses or tragedies even fifty years ago, they would likely have died. Before the advent of modern-day vaccines, millions would have no doubt died of smallpox, polio or other previously incurable diseases.

I think of these truths every time I talk to my friend Alda—a dear lady in my congregation who was diagnosed with kidney problems a few years ago. Like many of the people I interviewed for this book, Alda would not be alive today if not for the discovery and development of dialysis, a medical breakthrough that has saved millions of lives.

Although Alda goes to dialysis three times each week, and sits through a lengthy blood-purifying process that can take up to four hours each session, she has maintained a positive outlook on life and considers herself a healed individual.

"When I was first diagnosed with heart and kidney problems, I became depressed," she told me. "But I decided to read the Bible each morning and pray, trusting that God would help me to deal with my situation. When I had to go in for a CT scan one day, I had to pray that God would get me through my claustrophobia. I became aware of God helping me through that experience. Gradually, after that, and as the weeks passed, my cloud of depression lifted, and I was able to accept that my healing was ongoing and that God would be working through the dialysis treatments, even if I had to take them the rest of my life."

Amazingly, Alda doesn't see her dialysis treatments as a

"waste of time," but she actively uses her hours on the machine to work with her hands or read or write notes and letters to others. Sometimes she talks to the nurses and the medical technicians about their personal problems and tells them that she is praying for them. By focusing on other people, she finds that the dialysis not only passes much faster, but also provides her with an outlet to learn, to work and to assist others.

As Alda explains it, her healing is embodied in the attitude that she is able to accept what she cannot change and move on with her life. Although she often suffers from severe itching sensations, weakness and secondary symptoms associated with dialysis, she feels that she has been healed far beyond the physical, and she has used her situation to do good for others.

"I know I wouldn't be alive without dialysis," she told me. "But that's one of God's miracles, too."

Looking at physical healing in this way, we can see how God has given human beings the knowledge and the capability to heal one another. However, our ideas about healing often become so narrow, we simply don't see the miraculous healing work that is going on around us each day.

IS HEALING MIRACULOUS?

But how much of physical healing can be attributed to the miraculous? This is the question that most people ponder when reflecting on healing. People want to know if God can still heal when the best of medical science cannot. Often our faith turns to the hope of God's miracle cure when doctors tell us that there is nothing, medically, that can be done or when doctors tell a family that there is no hope.

Of course, people of faith always turn to God in times of need. That is the nature of our relationship with God. And when we are suffering, physically or otherwise, we turn to God for help.

We want to know: Does God heal today? Does God still work miracles? I believe the answer to both questions is *yes!*

In Frederick Buechner's little book, *Wishful Thinking: A Theological ABC,* he offers the following insights about healing:

> *Ever since the time of Jesus, healing has been a part of the Christian tradition. In this century it has usually been associated with religious quackery or the lunatic fringe, but as the psychosomatic dimension of disease has come to be taken more and more seriously by medical science it has regained some of its former respectability. How nice for God to have this support at last.*
>
> *If your approach to this kind of healing is less ideological and more empirical, you can always give it a try. Pray for it.*

If God doesn't seem to be giving you what you ask, maybe he's giving you something else.[7]

The insights here about God's healing touch are well noted. We do live in a time when healing has often been associated with the fringes of the church (though often with good reason). Anytime healing becomes a "show" (with emphasis upon the faith healer or the staging), or where people are asked to give money to support the healer, we can be sure there is something drastically wrong, even deceitful. But there can be no doubt that the church has by and large neglected the healing ministries that Jesus embodied.

I have found this to be true whenever the word "healing" is mentioned. People are naturally skeptical—yet hopeful. But underlying all of these insecurities associated with the word "healing" are hopes and needs that we can scarcely name.

Over the years, I've conducted very simple services of healing in the congregations I have served. These are not dramatically staged events (why should they be?) and I have always prepared these services, and punctuated them, with teaching about the biblical views of healing.

Without exception, I have always been blown away by the responses of the people—usually great numbers of them, who desire to be anointed with oil and to receive the prayers of the church. Not all of these requests (in fact, very few of them) are physical in nature. Many people want to be healed from emotional scars, from painful memories of the past, or to be restored with loved ones who have become estranged or bitter. Others desire to deepen their faith or to overcome a spiritual crisis in their lives.

It is noteworthy that through the long history of the church, oil has been associated with healing—along with the laying on of hands, confession of sin and prayer (see James 5:13–16). Although there may be some who will say that oil itself has healing properties, I have come to believe that the oil represents, very simply, the presence of Christ. The word "Christ" (Χριστός "Christos," in Greek, "Messiah," in Hebrew) means simply, "the anointed one"—and the oil, like the waters of baptism or the bread and cup of Communion, is a tangible reminder of the presence of God.

Most important are the connections with God and others represented by the physical touch (of oil and hands) and the openness of our lives represented by confession, pardon and prayer. These patterns and truths are deeply embodied in the life and ministry of Jesus, as we have already seen by exploring the Gospel accounts. The church becomes the body of Christ—a healing communion and movement—at precisely those points where we care for one another, bear one anothers' burdens and offer one another forgiveness, reconciliation and hope.

Sometimes, when we embody this love of Christ, the miraculous does occur. I have met several people who can claim such remarkable healings.

One man I know—David—received a miraculous healing several years ago when he was in his twenties. Inexplicably, David had slipped into a comatose state soon after performing a music concert. After being rushed to the hospital, he found himself trapped inside his own body—unable to move, speak or communicate in any way with those who had gathered around him.

Although David could hear the conversations, he could not open his eyes, lift a finger or move his lips. Realizing that he had a serious problem, David peacefully began to recite, in his mind, the words of several psalms that he had memorized, asking God to help him. Although he was in no pain himself, he could sense the pain of his family around him as they stood over his bed and wept.

At one point, he recalls his wife coming for a visit, holding his hand and telling him that it was all right for him to slip away into the arms of God. Inwardly, David wept, but no tears flowed from his body, and he had no way to communicate his condition to the doctors or hospital staff who were working so frantically to pull him back from the brink of death. Although he could not open his eyes or speak, David was at peace, and he wanted so desperately to tell everyone not to worry, not to struggle so valiantly for his life. For David, the greatest difficulty was realizing that the people who loved him were living in agony as they stood vigil beside his bed, as they prayed desperately that he might wake up.

Days passed. More prayers were offered. Many people were engaged in the battle for David's life.

And then one day he woke up. Just like that. As if he had emerged from a deep hibernation.

"We don't need to fear death," I've heard David say many times. "There is no doubt that God surrounds us with peace when our bodies are broken. What I learned from my healing is that the greatest agony remains with the living."

I think of David often whenever I consider God's healing touch. Medically, there was never any explanation given for his miraculous recovery. But those who know David can affirm that God's healing is real, indeed.

JOY AND HEALING

Moving more deeply into the healing grace of God, we can also see that joy and celebration go hand in hand with physical recovery, as we have noted when we talked about gratitude and

thanksgiving. In fact, humor and laughter may actually con-
tribute to our wholeness and well-being long before we are
healed, saving us from ailments and the physical stresses
brought on by depression, loneliness or despair. We cannot forget that healing is not simply the absence of disease, but is
found whenever we are "well" in body and spirit.

It is worth noting how often expressions of joy follow upon the
heels of healing in the Gospels. People jump up and down. Some
shout. Onlookers celebrate. To be made well or to recover from
an illness—even a common cold or a flu bug that forces us into
our beds—can often seem like being released from a prison.
When we are ill, our minds are not sound, and we long to be
released from physical discomfort. Here is where we most commonly experience joy.

But humor and laughter also have their place in wholeness. If
we want to be healed, we must learn to laugh, or to see the absurdities of our disease or predicament.

When my wife was going through her bout with breast cancer,
I recall a conversation with a fellow I met in the waiting room at
the hospital. His wife had come in for a round of chemotherapy
and had lost most of her hair. At one point, while we were talking
about the absurdities of cancer, he pulled a magazine out of his
coat pocket and showed me a catalogue of wigs. "My wife and I
have had a blast picking out a wig," he said. "I want her to be a
blonde. She wants to be a redhead. But we're going to compro-
mise and use the rainbow wig my kids wear on Halloween."

I found his humor uplifting, and I was certain that his wife
needed to laugh as much as he did. Later, when my wife and I
went in to our doctor to talk about breast implants, I had a bit of
fun suggesting that my wife could upgrade to a much larger
model. The surgeon even showed us several prototypes and
laughed when he told me, "You might want to talk her into
becoming a new woman."

Bernie Siegel, a famous medical doctor who has written several bestselling books, has commented frequently on the role of

humor and healing. He has seen firsthand how levity and laughter play a critical role, not only in healing, but in living longer and more fulfilling lives. He believes that a patient who can laugh at his or her condition stands a much better chance of recovery than a stolid individual who cannot find humor in the absurd.

Many studies, in fact, have shown that when we laugh, enzymes are released into our bodies that actually increase the rate of healing. Likewise, people who laugh suffer from far less depression and despair than people who take their situation or life more seriously.

From my own research, I have discovered that many of the "medicine men" or "shamans"—the healers who were prevalent in most early American Indian tribes—often dressed in bright and colorful costumes (much like circus clowns) and their art and demeanor was often intended to provoke laughter in the patient. Like many folk remedies or family cures, there is usually some sound medical or spiritual substance to these old ways. Perhaps, as many people realized in ages past, our laughter does often provoke healing properties, and, as many doctors will point out, the body can often heal itself if left alone. "First do no harm" is a mantra that many shamans and ancient physicians practiced, and we would do well to heed this advice today.

While I am not suggesting that people can simply give up medications and go with a prescription of laughter, I have known more than a few people who have found themselves living without pills soon after they discovered some new impetus for life or deepened their spirit of joy. One couple I know spends a few minutes each night, just before bed, reading jokes from a corny humor magazine. They have discovered that this simple element of laughter just before bed calms their spirits, helps them forget the troubles and worries that they might otherwise carry with them into sleep and helps them to awake refreshed in the morning, eager to embrace another day. It may sound overly simple, but it works for them.

There have been times that I, too, have found release from worries and cares simply by being in the company of a few seasoned cutups, and when I laugh, I discover that most of the seemingly insurmountable obstacles I believe I am facing don't seem so ominous or threatening after a good rib-splitter. I have to believe that the same is true when it comes to the healing properties of the body. Laughter, indeed, is often the best medicine. Amazingly, even a smile can make a difference in our physical well-being. As I mentioned in chapter 3, it takes many more muscles to frown than to smile. In other words, it takes far more effort, far more stress and strain, to frown and be unhappy than it does to smile. And whenever you or I smile at a stranger, chances are that person will smile back. Friendliness and levity spread much faster than anger and despair and give back a much greater return. I wonder how many incidents of road rage, how many fights and disagreements (some resulting in serious bodily injury) could simply be avoided if people disarmed each other with a smile or a kind word? Although it doesn't work every time, I have often found that a quick apology (even if I feel that I am in the right) or a quick joke can disarm an angry person and lead to better understanding. When people are expecting anger in return, or even retaliation, humor and levity can turn a situation upside down.

People who don't have much to smile about often need to smile most of all. A bit of laughter can also turn a despairing situation into one of healing and hope.

Not long ago, I drove across town to visit an elderly woman in a nursing home. Like so many places where people are confined to wheelchairs or beds, these places usually depress me, and I find that I must prepare myself to make these visits. But when I entered the nursing home that day, I was surprised to hear the sounds of laughter rising from the dining hall. There, perched in rows of padded wheelchairs and rolling beds, were many of the residents. They had gathered to listen to a young man who was singing country songs and telling jokes. The smiles on the faces of the people told me that they were having a wonderful time, and for that brief period, there wasn't a sick person in the room. Everyone, it seemed, had forgotten their surroundings and their situation.

The connections between levity and healing are real. And the ways in which humor can reach into the human spirit are amazingly bright.

One recent movie that does a fine job revealing these connections is the film *Patch Adams*—a story based on a real-life doctor who uses humor to bring hope and healing into the lives of sick and dying patients. The doctor, who is portrayed by Robin Williams in the movie, is misunderstood by both his peers and his patients, but his zany antics demonstrate how humor has the power to heal.

Thomas Addison, an English physician who practiced medicine in the early nineteenth century, noted that "health and cheerfulness mutually beget each other. Laughter breaks the gloom which depresses the mind and dampens the spirit."

When you and I consider the healing of the body, we might do well to look within ourselves and discover the healing grace of laughter, which is often described in the scriptures as joy—which is the awareness that, despite our circumstances, God is still the ruler.

Perhaps we may yet discover the healing properties of holy laughter and even incorporate them into our daily routines.

STAYING STRONG

As we have already seen through this exploration of healing, as Christians we are called to wholeness and holiness—of body, mind and spirit. When we abuse our bodies with too much food, too little exercise, destructive habits or self-defeating worries that we could give over to God, we are not practicing our faith in all of its fullness. On the other hand, when we take care of our bodies—eating right, exercising regularly and focusing on the needs of others—our bodies, as well as our spirits, are more vibrant, energized and whole. We are not only fit—we are well. That is what God created us to be. So often we focus on healing as the cure that comes after the sickness. But biblically speaking, we should focus on the cure that comes before the illness: being of sound body, mind and spirit. When we are connected with God, with others and with ourselves (including our past sorrows, defeats and sins), we live with a deeper fullness of life, and we can actually be of benefit to those needing the healing touch and presence of God's love—a love that Jesus said would flow through us by the power of the Holy Spirit.

Personal Inventory

As you take inventory of your own life, consider the status of your health. How are you doing in the wellness department?

- Do you pray each day, or meditate regularly upon scripture or the things of God?
- Where do you find release from the stresses of life?
- Are you eating well and exercising regularly?
- Are you finding enough sources of laughter and release in your life?
- Are there destructive habits that you need to rid from your life?
- What are the sources of your strength—mentally and emotionally?
- How is your philosophy of life lifting you up? How is it tearing you down?
- Are you living to work or working to live?
- What forms of relaxation and joy do you need to incorporate into your life?
- When will you MAKE THE NECESSARY CHANGES to become a healthier person.

Of course, some of these questions may be tougher than others. But as you take this inventory of your life, I hope you will do so with an open mind and willing heart. And don't forget—God will help you to make the necessary changes in your wellness program. Look to your family, also, for support.

Finally, lest we leave these matters thinking that ideas of health and wholeness are purely conjectures of the modern mind, we can look once again to the ancient, yet always contemporary, inspiration of the scriptures. Centuries ago, the psalmist sang a lovely song to the Lord that offers up all of the hope and promise of healing. These words, though written long ago, still resonate with the joy and promise of a whole life, flowing out of the existence of one who has found laughter and grace in the midst of life's difficulties and tragedies.

May we experience this same healing in our time.

Psalm 30

I will extol you, O Lord, for you have drawn me up,
And did not let my foes rejoice over me.
O Lord my God, I cried to you for help, and you have healed me.
O Lord, you brought up my soul from Sheol,
Restored me to life from among those gone down to the Pit.
Sing praises to the Lord, O you his faithful ones,
And give thanks to his holy name.
For his anger is but for a moment; his favor is for a lifetime.
Weeping may linger for the night, but joy comes with the morning.
To you, O Lord, I cried, and to the Lord I made supplication:
"What profit is there in my death, if I go down to the Pit?
Will the dust praise you? Will it tell of your faithfulness?
Hear, O Lord, and be gracious to me! O Lord, be my helper!"
You have turned my mourning into dancing;
You have taken off my sackcloth and clothed me with joy,
So that my soul may praise you and not be silent.
O Lord my God, I will give thanks to you forever.

6
STUDY GUIDE

When people hear the word "healing," they naturally think of "cure." But there is far more to physical healing. In addition to using all of the knowledge and expertise of medicine, we know that attitude, faith and community have an impact on our physical well-being. Laughter and joy are the natural responses to healing, but these attitudes can also help to prevent illness, too. Take a few minutes to consider these things, then ask:

- What is your philosophy of life? How does it affect your physical self?
- In what ways might medicine be a form of God's healing touch?
- In what ways is medicine (at least as we know it now) not sufficient to address the complexity of human illness and need?
- How do you personally use medical knowledge and faith in your understanding of wellness?
- What miracles of bodily healing have you witnessed?
- What do you think of the author's assertion that faith and medicine (though often strange bedfellows) were evident in the healing ministry of Jesus?
- What practices or attitudes have shaped your wellness program?

Read Mark 2:1–12 and John 9:1–34, then ask: What strikes you as helpful in these healing stories? What other factors—other than God's single power—might have contributed to these healings? What insights have you gleaned from previous chapters that offer new light to these accounts of healing?

Close your time by taking the personal inventory found at the end of the chapter.

Prayer: Healing God, you have created our bodies from the dust of the earth. You formed us in our mothers' wombs. You know everything about us—including our health, our illnesses and our patterns of behavior. We pray that you will give us not only healthy bodies, but healthy minds and spirits as well. For we know that we are never well unless we are whole inside. We do pray for those who need your healing touch upon their bodies today, and we pray for ourselves, that you would bless us with long and productive lives, for your kingdom's sake. Amen.

CHAPTER 7

Resurrection Healing: Experiencing the Promise of New Life

So it is with the resurrection of the dead. What is sown is perishable, what is raised is imperishable. It is sown in dishonor, it is raised in glory. It is sown in weakness, it is raised in power. It is sown a physical body, it is raised a spiritual body. If there is a physical body, there is also a spiritual body.

—1 Corinthians 15:42–44

The last enemy to be destroyed is death.

—1 Corinthians 15:26

*T*his chapter may seem superfluous or contradictory to many people. After all, if one is writing about healing and wellness and life, what sense are we to make of the idea that our ultimate healing is realized only at the time of death? How can we speak of healing and death at the same time?

To many, the idea of resurrection healing may seem strange. And then again, it may be the most biblical idea that one will encounter anywhere in this book.

This is because the scriptures do indeed speak of our deaths as God's ultimate healing. In fact, the Gospels, and particularly Paul's letters to the churches, are chock-full of these juicy theological tidbits, this odd mixture of life and death talk that speaks both of our life now—which is often regarded as weak or incomplete—and the life to come, which is often referred to as life eternal, the abundant life or the completed work of God's grace. But I suppose, as the apostle Paul himself realized, we can never know the fullness of God's power and grace until we come to grips with the reality of our own demise. For the truth is . . . we are all going to die.

How odd it has always seemed to me that, even in the church, we often gloss over this inescapable fact—or talk around the issue of healing and wholeness—as if death were not a part of our human experience. Sometimes, we have difficulty saying the word "death"—and so we speak of "passing on" or "going on" or "crossing over." Or we live as if death is not a possibility, or deny that death holds any power in our world, or we grow numb to the reality of our mortality by immersing ourselves in fake images of death or violence that come to us via the television or movies. Many people simply choose to live as if this life has no boundaries—no beginning and end—and thus they lose the significance and the purpose behind the life God has given us.

Life, indeed, is a gift. And this gift can be snatched from us at any time. That is why the Christian faith teaches us to cherish each other, to treasure our days while we still have them and to count each day as a blessing from God.

This is why the idea of healing and death are not polar opposites, as many might assume. But rather, they go hand in hand.

A quick reality check through the scriptures can help us here.

In the preceding chapters we looked at many forms of healing—emotional, spiritual, social and otherwise. We have read of the healing of many people. We have seen how Jesus touched them and brought them out of darkness into light, or out of a sterile world of silence into a life filled with the sound of God's joy. But in every instance, in every healing, we cannot overlook the fact that there was also a death.

Blind Bartimaeus was healed. He received his sight. But he eventually died. The eyes that Jesus touched were darkened once again.

The Samaritan woman at the well may have renewed her life. But she died. So did all of the neighbors who had attended to her witness.

The miraculous healings witnessed in the Acts of the Apostles (see Acts 3:1–9; 9:36–43; 19:11–12) were temporary healings. All of the people who received their sight or their hearing or their ability to walk eventually succumbed to illness, to the weakness of the flesh, and they died.

These are often the realities that we fail to see when we are talking about healing. All people who have received a healing will someday die. And when we look at the life of Jesus, we see that he also was weak in the flesh, for his body was tortured and broken, and he breathed his last on a cross. These truths about Jesus cannot be ignored, for in him we see the path and the realities that we all must face. Jesus suffered. And he said that his followers would suffer. Jesus died. And he said that his followers would also be persecuted and would die.

But herein lies the most wonderful truth: although our bodies will perish, we have confidence and hope that God will give us an imperishable body; and even as God raised Jesus from the dead, we too shall be raised (John 6:35–40; 1 Cor. 15:53–57).

Resurrection, then, is our ultimate healing. For although we shall wither and die, leaving behind unfinished business, all of our relationships and loves, even our unfulfilled human hopes and dreams, God will take what we cannot complete, what we cannot accomplish on our own, and raise us to new life. Whatever healings and blessings we have received, these, too, will become part of our human predicament when we die. But faith in Christ offers us the promise that even though we die, in Christ we shall be raised (Rom. 8:9–11; Eph. 4:2–10).

Often when we speak of healing within the Christian tradition, we overlook the realities of death or pretend that ultimately healing of the body is all that matters. But theologically, we have seen how a person may not receive a physical healing (may not receive sight or hearing or a cure from cancer) and yet may be healed. This may seem an odd assertion, especially for many in the church, but it is quite biblical.

In fact, the apostle Paul himself spoke eloquently of this reality when, in writing his bright and moving letter to the church at Philippi, he said: "Christ will be exalted now as always in my body, whether by life or by death. For to me, living is Christ and dying is gain" (Phil. 1:20–21). We can see then that bodily healing is not always the sign of God's promise and blessing. There are many people who are sick or who must live with pain and discomfort or uncertainty of health who are equally as faithful—if not more so—than those who live healthy, pain-free lives. A person's illness or aging body is ultimately healed only through death and being raised to new life in Christ.

I have hoped for this promise of healing many times in my ministry, especially when I have stood beside the beds of dying friends and family members, praying, not for their physical healing but for God's promise of new life beyond the grave. This hope is especially powerful and is also a witness to our faith in Christ. In fact, this is our greatest hope, for nothing in this life (outside of faith, hope and love—1 Cor. 13:13) will abide for eternity. Everything else will pass away.

Some years ago, I was serving a congregation that offered me a powerful testimony to the truth of resurrection healing. A dear woman in the congregation named Judy had been diagnosed with cancer. For weeks, months even, we surrounded Judy with prayers for her healing and full recovery. Vigils were organized. Meals were coordinated and assistance was given to her husband and children. But Judy's condition continued to spiral downward. Her body weakened even, as it seemed, her spirit grew strong and more resilient.

Treatments of every kind were administered. Experimental drugs were tried. And it seemed that the congregation was being swept up in the drama of Judy's battle. Some people organized a fund-raiser for her children's schooling. Others spent evenings with her in the hospital. She was the topic of much discussion.

Everyone, it seemed, who knew Judy was touched by her life in some way. But through it all, we held out the hope that Judy might be healed of her disease and be able to continue her journey of faith and enjoy the blessings of her family and friends. As the weeks passed, however, Judy grew weaker and eventually began to open up and speak of her death—not as some distant, unfathomable end, but as a reality and a new beginning.

Once, during one of my visits with Judy, she began to speak of her faith in a very bold way. "I know I'm not going to live much longer," she said. "But I'm at peace. I know I'm not going to get well, but I believe that my death will be a doorway to a new life with God. I believe this is how God is going to heal me."

One day, not long after this conversation, a call arrived informing me that Judy was not expected to live through the night. Once again, we were touched by her spirit. And, even though she died later that night, there was the feeling that God had indeed answered our prayers for Judy's healing. Death was not the end, but a new beginning for Judy in the arms of Jesus.

I will come back to Judy later in this chapter, for the end of her life also marked the beginning of some awesome events. For there is no doubt that Judy's passing had a deep impact on the lives of many.

FROM HERE TO ETERNITY

If the scriptures speak of death as a reality, then we need not doubt that death will at last lay claim to each of us. But the Gospel of Christ tells us that death will not have the final word. This is the meaning of resurrection, and it is why the scriptures, especially the New Testament, speaks so eloquently of death as an enemy of God (1 Cor. 15:26). Saying that death is real is not the same as saying that God created death or that God causes our death.

This distinction is important, because, as we explored in our discussion of theological healing, how we see death does play a role in how we live life. We can see God as the arbiter of endings or as the author of beginnings. And if we see God as a creator who is making all things new, then we can affirm with St. Paul that nothing can separate us from the love of God, "neither death, nor life, nor angels, nor rulers, nor things present, nor things to come, nor powers, nor height, nor depth, nor anything else in all creation, will be able to separate us from the love of God in Christ Jesus our Lord" (Rom. 8:38–39).

Certainly our times are in God's hands—and our beginnings, as well as our endings, are held within the mystery of God's providence. And yet we live and move and have our being within the mystery of God's grace as well. Death, like birth, is a part of the mystery of life: this wondrous and blessed adventure that will bring us, at last, into the fullness of God's glory.

Our final healing takes place within the mystery of God's will—a mystery that we will explore more fully in the final chapter. This mystery is one of the reasons why we ask our most penetrating questions around the wonder of God's providence.

Why was *this* person healed and not *that* person?

Does prayer *really* change anything?

Why does God allow illness and death, if he could eradicate such suffering from the earth?

Why can't we arrive at solid answers to these difficult questions?

Surely every person of faith has wondered about such things. And these are the questions people have asked for centuries. And yet, within the questions themselves, perhaps we can arrive at a place where, although we may not have the answers, we may experience God's presence and peace in a very profound way.

Not long after I began serving as a student chaplain in a large North Carolina hospital many years ago, I encountered such questions on an almost daily basis. But the questions were not always directed at God, and did not always have a theological bent. Sometimes the questions were thrown at doctors or nurses. Sometimes the questions came to family members. And there were also times when people popped questions at the young chaplain.

One powerful memory centers on a conversation I had with a fellow who was dying of congestive heart failure. He was not a particularly old man, and although I can see his face, I have long since forgotten his name. As he lay in the hospital bed, hooked to a tangle of wires and tubes and monitors, sometimes gasping for breath, he opened his life to me and shared some of his deepest fears and doubts.

"I have a lot of regrets in my life," he told me. "I've always fancied myself a rather religious man. But now that I have this condition, I feel like I've wasted so much of my life. I wish I had made more of an effort in the church—you know—to help others. I wish I had done more with my family. I feel like God has given me so much and I've wasted the blessing. I don't see how God can accept someone who has wasted so much of his life."

"You know," I answered, "sometimes we Christians get confused about the Gospel. We think that everything depends upon what we do or what we don't do. And we forget that this isn't the Gospel message at all."

He looked at me, a bit confused to be sure, but then waited for me to offer him some good news. "The message of Christ's love," I continued, "centers on God's ability to love us, even when we are unfaithful and weak. The Gospel of Jesus is not about what we have done for God, but about what God has done for us.

"You're right," I told him. "You are unworthy to be loved by God
. . . just as I am. But God loves us anyway. Isn't that what you
have learned?"

He smiled faintly. "Yes," he whispered. "I guess I forgot about
that."

There was a moment of silence and then he spoke again. "I
guess since God has lived with me so far, God will take me as I
am now."

Gospel. Good news. Resurrection!

He gave a great sigh, closed his eyes and asked me to pray
with him. I have no doubt that this man found God's peace, and
God's ultimate healing, through his death.

ACCEPTING GOD'S ULTIMATE HEALING

The most difficult aspect of resurrection healing, of course, is
the thought of dying. The very idea of ceasing to exist causes us
great consternation (which is why, I suppose, that so many don't
think about, or plan for, their deaths at all).

But the scriptures remind us that we cannot rise with Christ
until we first die with him. This dying, however, does not take
place at the moment of death, but begins at the point where we
are willing to take up our cross, each day, and follow the Lord.
Long ago, Jesus instructed the disciples about death and new life
when he said: "If any want to become my followers, let them deny
themselves and take up their cross daily and follow me. For those
who want to save their life will lose it, and those who lose their
life for my sake will save it" (Luke 9:23–24).

Likewise, the apostle Paul, in writing to the church at Corinth
about the resurrection, talks of this dying and rising in the following manner: "But in fact, Christ has been raised from the
dead, the first fruits of those who have died. For since death came
through a human being, the resurrection of the dead has come
through a human being; for as all die in Adam, so all will be made

alive in Christ. I die every day!" (1 Cor. 15:20–22, 31).

Of course, there is a mystery to this dying and rising in Christ. But it is a mystery born of the life we choose to live each day—a cruciform life—a life that is dedicated to the service of others, love of our neighbor and sacrifice for the sake of the kingdom and the glory of God. To live a cruciform life is to die each day in Christ and to be raised anew in his power and strength, so that, at the end of our days, we go from glory to glory, trusting that God will raise us to new life and transform our mortal frames into glorified bodies. That is ultimate healing.

Of course, we struggle to remember this aspect of the Gospel in our daily lives. We are weighed down with concerns, easily distracted by the enticements of the senses and the desires of our hearts. Most of the time, we fail to see the ways that we are dying and rising in Christ each day. But it is only by God's grace and strength that we learn to trust God in our manner of living.

When we are sick or afflicted—or struggling with the illness of a loved one—it is often difficult to look past the illness itself and see God's goodness. Or perhaps our attentions and hopes are attached only to the interventions of medicine or a prayer for bodily healing. We find it difficult to look past the illness itself and see that there is a greater healing yet to come—a healing that is not temporary, but eternal.

There are many ways that we witness this lack of trust in our lives—this lack of trust in God's providence and goodness. And often these doubts can attach themselves to moments when we experience pain or need.

I recall an afternoon, a few years ago, when I happened to be at home recovering from the flu. My recovery was made all the more difficult because of some pressing issues that I was facing, and I felt that I didn't really have the time to rest and regain my strength (and yet I wasn't going to get well unless I allowed myself—mentally, emotionally and otherwise—the space to rest).

Lying on the couch that day, I was flipping through the television channels when I happened upon a healing service that was being conducted in a giant auditorium by a well-known "faith healer." I watched as one person after another came forward to receive the touch. Nearly all of them immediately announced that they were healed—having received sight, hearing or a pain-free mobility.

Finally, near the end of the event, a woman of considerable age was brought onto the stage—actually wheeled onto the stage by her family—still lying in a hospital bed, her body propped at a thirty-degree angle. Her eyes were closed, her breathing shallow, and it was apparent that she was nonresponsive. One person in her family announced that she was ninety years old, and that they were requesting that God "heal her and allow her to rise from her bed and walk."

It was instantly obvious that the faith healer had met his match. In fact, unlike the other people who had entered the stage on their own, here was a woman nearing the end of life who was completely nonresponsive, nearly comatose and who could not speak for herself. I watched in horror as the evangelist leaned over her body, prayed that she might rise and walk and then announced weakly, "Of course, sometimes God doesn't give us a miracle all at once. These things take time."

There was, of course, absolutely no physical change in the dear woman—and the family was ushered off of the stage quickly. Although I might have agreed with the final statement by the evangelist (that much in life does take time), I was confused by his apparent unwillingness or inability to see that this woman was at the end of her life. To pray that she would rise and walk was both unrealistic and confusing. Wouldn't a better prayer have consisted of words for God's presence, asking that God might be made known to the woman in her comatose state? Wouldn't it have been more faithful to pray that her family would continue to surround her with love and prayer, and that they might hope for, and accept, her peaceful death into God's glory?

I suppose that to many this attitude may seem fatalistic. But as the apostle Paul said centuries ago, "For to me, living is Christ and dying is gain" (Phil. 1:21). We are not a fatalistic people because we believe in the ultimate healing of God through death and resurrection. Rather, we are hopeful, trusting that God can transform what is weak and dying into that which is glorious and eternal.

Accepting this good news, however, is not easy—and apparently not easy for faith healers, either. So often, our attachments to the temporary—even a temporary healing—can keep us from seeing and celebrating the wonderful news of Easter.

Christ is risen! And because he lives, we shall live also.

A FINAL BLESSING

These thoughts bring me back to God's blessings that are offered to us without price each day and that sustain us through life's deepest hardships and darkest hours. When we have reached that stage of life when even our living is painful to us, when we are no longer able, in our weakness, to enjoy the bounty and beauty of life, let us not give up on the promises of God, but hold fast to them, setting our hearts and minds on things yet to come. If God can create all things new, then God can make us new as well, and give us the strength to walk with Christ through his suffering.

Perhaps if we have lost anything in the church, we have lost the ability to comprehend the significance of death. In our culture, we do all that we can to avoid it (or we dramatize it in ways that are neither healthy nor realistic). Few people, I think, ever truly grasp the idea of death's blessing (not something we choose for ourselves, but a moment that God chooses for our ultimate healing and transformation).

As a pastor, I am grateful whenever I am able to be with a family through this transformation, and to witness the blessing (though extremely painful!) of God's final promise.

Which brings me back around to Judy. Remember her story, earlier in this chapter?

During those final hours of Judy's life, there is no doubt that she was surrounded by love—a love born of family and of God. In fact, her Sunday school class had come to gather around her bed during those final hours to pray (not for her recovery any longer, but that God would receive her in the grace of Jesus). Eventually, someone suggested that the class encircle her bed and sing. And we did.

It was a few days before Christmas, and the songs that filled our thoughts were those of angels and shepherds, of Mary and Joseph and the love that came down from heaven into a broken world. We sang, "Hark the herald angels sing, glory to the new-born king," and I thought: indeed, Christ is born in us, not only in our living, but also in our deaths, and this is enough.

And when we sang "O Little Town of Bethlehem" and came to the words of the final stanza, "O holy child of Bethlehem, descend to us, we pray; cast out our sin and enter in, be born in us today," it was as if God were opening the gates of heaven and revealing to each of us the mystery of everlasting love in the welcoming of Judy's spirit.

As we exited her room that evening, however, there was an inexplicable warmth, an overflowing of love, in the hospital hall-ways. At one point, a young nurse approached our little group and thanked us. She added: "Thank you for reminding me that God can enter into a place like this. And thank you for helping to make God's love real."

Later that night, Judy slipped away peacefully to God.

In the coming weeks, however—long after the aura of Christmas had passed—there were evidences of God's transform-ing power through Judy's witness and her life. When Judy died, she left behind many roles in the church—places of service and dedication that she had filled for years. One by one, people stepped forward to take up those crosses of service and to carry the church forth in ministry. Many of the hospital staff who had attended to Judy during her illness not only came to her funeral service, but also shared their insights into Judy's faith and per-severance and what she had meant to them.

At the end of her life, Judy had a profound impact on others—

even as she had during her lifetime.

Likewise, you and I can never underestimate the transforming power of the lives we live and the witness that may be revealed, ultimately, through our deaths. This transforming power is not of our own, but comes from God, who creates all things new.

That is why we sing, "He lives!" on Easter morning and why we live in a faith and hope that God's healing is not merely a temporary blessing, but an eternal joy.

7
STUDY GUIDE

We cannot forget that all cures are ultimately ineffective, for no amount of curing can change our ultimate end. The Gospel, however, does not sugarcoat death, but proclaims our ultimate healing and transformation through it. Our end is a new beginning, for God gives us a new body fit for eternity. Consider this good news in your life and the message of resurrection healing as it relates to your pain and need. Then ask:

- Why is death often a difficult subject to talk about? How do we ignore this reality in our culture? In the church?
- In what ways does the reality of death (if even only subliminally recognized) affect how we live our lives?
- How might our beliefs in the world to come affect our health and well-being (positively or negatively)?
- In what ways is the promise of resurrection the ultimate form of healing?
- Why do you think people might have difficulty accepting death, even when a serious illness reduces the quality of life?
- What do you believe about death? About resurrection? About this form of healing?

Read 1 Corinthians 15. Then ask: What does this passage say about resurrection as a form of bodily healing? How might resurrection also heal us socially, relationally or emotionally? Where do we see evidences of God's resurrection healing in our world? In the church?

Prayer: Dear God, you have shown us a path of suffering, death and resurrection through your Son, Jesus. By faith, we follow him through this same pathway into life eternal. Grant that our faith may be such that we do not deny the realities of death, or hide from it, but trust in your grace and goodness to see us through all of our ends, as well as our new beginnings. Our lives are hidden in your love and faithfulness, and we give you thanks. Amen.

CHAPTER 8

Healing and Theodicy: Struggling to Find God's Love in Our Pain

Then Job answered the Lord: "I know that you can do all things, and that no purpose of yours can be thwarted. 'Who is this that hides counsel without knowledge?' Therefore I have uttered what I did not understand, things too wonderful for me, which I did not know."

—Job 42:1–3

With all wisdom and insight he has made known to us the mystery of his will, according to his good pleasure that he set forth in Christ, as a plan for the fullness of time, to gather up all things in him, things in heaven and things on earth.

—Ephesians 1:8–10

*F*or many, "theodicy" may be a new word. But it is an ancient question. At its heart, theodicy is simply the age-old problem of human pain joined to faith in God. Theodicy is that small piece of faith that causes us to ask questions like:

Why, if God is all-powerful and all-loving, does God allow evil and suffering to exist?

Why doesn't a God who can do anything simply eradicate pain and misery in the world?

How can we make sense of suffering within the context of a loving and gracious God?

If God created all things, and is all-knowing, then isn't the existence of evil and suffering in the world at least indirectly caused by God?

What does the suffering and death of Jesus have to tell us about God's relationship with pain and our ultimate redemption?

Regardless of how people ask the questions, this final chapter holds importance for the exploration of healing and wholeness—an exploration that we have already undertaken, in part, in the preceding chapters. A person asking, "Why has God allowed this illness to happen to me?" is asking a question about God's fairness and justice. A person who asks, "Why didn't God heal my friend?" is asking a question about God's presence or power.

Of course, such questions are usually tied to the problem of pain, or more specifically, to those moments when we feel pain. Our questions arise from our difficulties, our hope that God might come to our aid or might deliver us from some calamity.

Job dredged up an abundance of these questions about God's fairness and mercy—and in the end received no answers. At the climax of the story, God merely demonstrates to Job the limitations and weaknesses of human knowledge. "Where were you when I created the world?" God asks (Job 38:4).

Likewise, the prophet Habakkuk asked, "O Lord, how long

shall I cry for help, and you will not listen?" (Hab. 1:2). But God's answer came only in the form of parables, leaving the prophet to wrestle with his initial quandary.

And we cannot forget that Jesus himself asked these penetrating questions also. In the garden on the night before his crucifixion, he knelt and prayed fervently that God might remove the cup of suffering from him, but then prayed, "yet not what I want, but what you want" (Matt. 26:39). On the cross, Jesus also experienced the loneliness and horror of imminent death when he cried out the question: "My God, my God, why have you forsaken me?" (Matt. 27:46).

Are there answers to such questions? Are there answers to the problems of our pain, our self-destructiveness, our questions about God's presence and justice?

I am not sure. But I am convinced that a deeper look at the life and death of Jesus can help us to understand God's love, and to understand the promise of God's presence in the midst of our suffering—even when we have doubts and questions.

First, when we look at Jesus, we see that God has drawn near to us in the form of a suffering servant. Jesus was born as we are—entering a suffering and broken world, full of the same heartbreak and limitations as you and I experience. His presence in the world as Emmanuel ("God with us," as the name means in Hebrew or Aramaic) points us to a God who cares deeply for the suffering of humanity, a God who has chosen to walk alongside us—not above us or beyond us—and to help us bear the difficulties and afflictions of life.

That Jesus touched people and healed them (consider again all of the *forms* of these healings!) is also indicative of God's love and offers witness to God's desire that we be whole people, and that we take responsibility for our own lives and our well-being. Like the prophets before him, Jesus also proclaimed that there was good news in the forgiveness of sins, and he asked that we turn away from those paths that lead to suffering and destruction (of which there are many) and walk with God down the narrow path of serving others in justice and in love. When we do these things, we experience true peace.

Finally, the suffering of Jesus and his death on the cross represent a demonstrative act of God's redemptive power. Jesus experienced great suffering (as there is great suffering in the world) and death (as we will all experience death), but was, nevertheless, faithful until the end. This faithfulness of Jesus—even through suffering and death—is how the apostle Paul describes the atoning work of God. God was present in Christ, working through his faithfulness, his pain and his death, in such a manner that you and I may know God's abiding presence and redemption as well. This awesome display of redemption—a salvation wrought through Christ's suffering, death and resurrection—is described eloquently in an early Christian hymn:

Christ was truly God.
But he did not remain equal with God.
He gave up everything and became a slave,
When he became like one of us.
Christ was humble.
He obeyed God and even died on a cross.
Then God gave Christ the highest place and honored his name
    above all others.
So at the name of Jesus everyone will bow down,
Those in heaven, on earth, and under the earth.
And to the glory of God the Father everyone will openly agree,
"Jesus Christ is Lord." (Phil. 2:6–11, Contemporary English
    Version [CEV])

I offer these thoughts about Jesus himself, because as we consider the forms of our own sufferings and earthly pains, we may find some answers to our questions about illness and heartache through his faithful witness and, ultimately, through our faithfulness to God and to each other. No doubt, we will not understand the mystery of pain this side of heaven, but through Jesus we can see the greatness and power of God, who walks with us on the mountains and through the valleys, and offers us eternal healing.

A QUESTION OF HEALING

As a pastor, I have often witnessed people's pain and disillusionment. More specifically, there have been many times when people have hoped and prayed for God's healing (either for themselves or for others) only to experience the disappointment of loss. Death, of course, is a loss. Through death, we are separated from those we love. We must learn to travel on—often with greater difficulties and heartaches—through the high waters and the obstacles of life. Death also represents the end of our striving, our work, our connections, our earthly dreams and our personal goals. Death is the loss of identity, since we measure the knowledge of ourselves, and others, through the relationships we share, the bodies we *are* and the love we extend to one another. Death snatches all of this, and more, from us.

Death also accounts for the questions we have in relation to God's presence and power.

As a teenager, I recall spending much time in a Sunday school class one winter discussing questions about the unexpected deaths of some friends in our congregation—friends who had been killed in car accidents or died suddenly from severe illnesses. "Why did God allow it to happen?" some asked. "Why didn't God intervene?" others wondered.

In the end, we are left with more questions than answers, especially as our faith deepens and we begin to see that life and faith do not always provide neatly detailed blueprints. The Bible itself also reflects these many questions and does not always provide slick or pat answers to the complexities we often experience.

Philip Gulley, in his bestselling book *Front Porch Tales,* recounts an event in his early life when he learned about the death of his best friend, Tim, who had been killed by a drunk driver. For him, Tim's death represented a question of God's justice: Why does a drunken driver die of old age when a never-hurt-a-flea young man barely sees twenty?[8]

Phil Gulley, in his marvelous essay, explains that he has yet to arrive at an answer to that question, but as a young man, he was equally threatened by the people who tried to explain the reasons for his friend's death, as if they had some secret knowledge about the mysteries of life or knew the mind of God. He preferred, rather, that these well-meaning people would go away, would leave him to his own struggle with death and would not attempt to explain the unexplainable.

There is wisdom here. For one of the most horrible mistakes we can make is when we attempt to explain why a death has occurred, or attempt to help a person who is grieving by offering a trite cliché about God's will or a simplistic explanation for a deeply personal tragedy. If Jesus had questions about God's presence and justice in his suffering, then surely we will, too!

These same questions hold true when we turn our attentions to God's healing touch. There is a mystery to God's healing that, obviously, we cannot fully explain. That is why, in part, there is much difference of opinion about the miraculous or about the place of faith and hopefulness in relation to medical science. In the same way, our beliefs about healing often return to the questions about God's silence, or the seeming absence of God's healing touch in the lives of people who are starving or suffering from serious and undeserved illness or dying of curable diseases in faraway lands. Chances are, we have never heard of someone being cured of Parkinson's disease, Lou Gehrig's disease, AIDS or from horrible injuries such as a severed spine. And as we venture further into the spiritual complexity of our lives, we often see that in many ways we are responsible for our own illnesses and tragedies, yet we wonder why God doesn't shield us from ourselves. There are days when we realize that we are our own worst enemies and that much of the human suffering in the world is, indeed, brought about by human sinfulness and limitation.

On the other hand, sometimes we want to know why God didn't answer our prayers for a loved one's healing or deliver a friend from a painful death. We are as uncertain in the answers to these dead-end questions as we are in answering the unexplainable personal transformations or the miraculous medical outcomes.

Which may bring us full circle to where we began: standing, perhaps, in awe of what God *does* do for us and asking the more penetrating questions about the mysteries of God's redeeming grace.

I think of these things as I ponder the wonder of Brandon Connor. Before his birth, doctor's discovered a lump growing near his spine, and after he was born, he was diagnosed with neuro-blastoma—one of the deadliest of childhood cancers. For more than two years, doctors monitored the growth of this tumor in Brandon's body, and soon after his second birthday, his parents decided to take him to the University of California, San Francisco, to undergo a very risky surgery to remove the cancerous growth. However, on the eve of his surgery, the surgeons examined a recent set of X-rays and discovered that the growth had vanished.

Cases like Brandon's—as well as Tim Kaczmarek's, whose heart repaired itself, or Stacey Perotta's, a young lady who lived through rounds of chemotherapy to beat a rare form of softball-sized cancer—are mystifying to doctors, as well as to their families and the patients themselves.[9] Some might explain these miracles in scientific terms—pointing out the benefits of early detection or the human body's natural ability to heal itself. Others might point to misdiagnoses. Likewise, the patient's attitude and outlook can be a factor, as can "beating the odds."

However, as many leading physicians often recognize, medical science needs to leave a door open for faith and self-cure when it comes to illnesses. While medicine is often miraculous in itself, there are some outcomes that cannot be explained in purely medical terms. And so we speak of miracles of God.

But the miracles themselves lead us around again to the questions. And we know that it is often difficult to speak of miracles or healing when other people continue to suffer and die.

We know, for instance, that not all children are born healthy. Not all children who are diagnosed with tumors (such as Brandon) go on to live. There are other situations that have entirely different outcomes—births filled with deep sadness, a sense of loss or inexpressible pain. There is no one lesson we can draw from these miraculous outcomes, for we know that not all births or heart defects or lives have wonderful transformations just because we pray for that outcome or wish it to be so. But, then, neither is life intrinsically fair, for we are all born with differing gifts, abilities, appearances, deficiencies and handicaps.

Despite these stark realities, however, life is still full of the mystery and majesty of God, and most of the time, I am convinced we miss the miraculous work of God that is going on around us each day through medical science, through support groups, through prayer circles, and through churches and synagogues and other communities of faith. Life is awesome and filled with many evidences of healing and transformation.

God, who is a creator, is continually making all things new—and, indeed, is transforming the very substance of our lives, day by day, whether we are aware of his presence or not. *Seeing* God's activity requires faith. And asking the right questions always leads us back to God.

Although we are not the first people to ask such deep and amazing questions, it is amazing how often we find words of insight and comfort in the Bible. The scriptures always seem fresh in this way, as if words written centuries ago can somehow speak to our situations and our circumstances today.

The Psalms are especially rich with these insightful prayers. And one of the most penetrating psalms (for our purposes here) can be found in the words of Psalm 13.

Here is my own paraphrase of this beautiful expression of faith and the questions that continue to bridge the gap between yesterday and today and forever.

Psalm 13

How long will you forget about me, Lord?
How long are you going to remain a mystery?
How long will I have to endure this pain,
And experience sorrow, day after day?
How long will you allow my enemies to triumph over me?
Consider all these questions and answer me. You are my God!
Open my eyes and show me the way, or I will surely die,
And then my enemy will say, "I am the victor!"
And my foes will shout for joy because I am defeated.
But I have always trusted in your unwavering love
And I'm going to keep on rejoicing in your salvation.
I will sing to you, Lord, because you have healed me and given
me all things.

FINAL THOUGHTS

As we have seen in the previous chapters, we are, in so many
ways, participants in our own healing. Although God is, ultimately, the healer, our choices and decisions and attitudes have
great bearing on our journey and destination into wholeness.

In effect, the problems of our pain are raised to higher levels
when we refuse to take responsibility for, or to initiate movement
toward, our own well-being. Inasmuch as we have questions
about God's justice and power, we may also do well to ask ourselves the most penetrating questions of all:

*Am I taking action now to make myself a more wholesome per-
son—in body, mind and spirit?*

*Are there habits, needs or cravings that have taken control of
my life—and that are causing me unnecessary pain and illness?*

*Where can I change my behavior and attitudes so that I might
become a healthy person?*

*In what ways might I be responsible for my own sickness—and
likewise, my own healing?*

Where in my life am I willing to open myself to God's healing touch?

As we ask these questions of ourselves and our situations, we can see that they draw us back to where we began this study: understanding the difference between healing and wholeness. Our goal as faithful people is to be whole—healthy in our relationships, healthy in our minds, and healthy in our bodies and habits. When we strive for health, we are already on the way to healing! To be healed is to be healthy (and not just physically). Health is the state of body, mind and spirit that embodies our wholeness.

Of course, even with our highest and best efforts, we are still imperfect people. We are flawed. And that is where God's grace makes all the difference in the world.

When we examine the final triumph of Jesus through his suffering and death, we see that there is a message here for each of us—in fact, for the whole world. The good news of the tragedy of Jesus is this: only God can transform pain and death. God can take what is bad or evil and transform it into goodness and redemption. This is the message of the cross. And that is why Christians have always called the day of crucifixion Good Friday—although in its essence, there was nothing good or befitting in the suffering and death of the Christ.

But God can transform death into life, which is why the Gospel affirms that death is the final step of our redemption—a process of salvation that is ongoing during our lifetimes. Through death, in fact, God gives us the inheritance of eternal life—transforming all of our suffering and tragedy into triumph.

The apostle Paul used the analogy of a seed to describe this final healing when he wrote: "What is sown is perishable, what is raised is imperishable. It is sown in dishonor, it is raised in glory. It is sown in weakness, it is raised in power" (1 Cor. 15:42–43).

The message of hope and healing is that God is able to transform our weakness into glory. God can transform our sufferings into joy. God can turn our wounds into crowns. And God can transform our deaths into resurrection victories.

Although we may not have all the answers to our questions, we can understand that God is on our side—and not against us. God is love, and life and hope. Whatever obstacles and challenges we may face in life, God can help us to be healed of our infirmities, and God can forgive our sins and strengthen the weaknesses in our lives.

That is God's healing touch.

8
STUDY GUIDE

F aith is not the absence of questions. Faith is trusting in God, even when we don't know the answers. No study of healing would be complete without acknowledging that we cannot fully explain the miraculous or the reasons why some are healed and others are not. Life is complex. And so are the questions we sometimes ask of God and of others. Take a few moments to reflect on your questions and then write a few down. After a few moments, proceed with the following:

• What questions would you ask God regarding healing?
• How might the life, death and resurrection of Jesus help us to deal with our own pain and uncertainties?
• Are there people you have known who have been healed? Are there people you know who may not have been healed?
• Where do you find strength when you must deal with illness, death or separation?
• What words of the Bible provide comfort to you in times of distress?

Go back and read the questions that are found at the end of this chapter. Try to answer them in your own mind or with the group, and then read Psalm 13. Ask: What questions can be found in this psalm? In what ways are they pertinent for today? Why do you think the psalmist did not answer the questions? What do you find helpful in this psalm?

Prayer: God, you continue to abide with us through all of the uncertainties of life. You help us in our times of distress and even bear with us through our doubts and questions. We do want to be healed, however, and we continue to pray that your will may be done. And so we pray that your will may be done today in our lives—and through all of our days—in our living, in our dying and in our rising to new life. Amen.

NOTES

Introduction

1 Lischer, Richard. *Open Secrets,* 154–63. New York: Doubleday, 2001. I am indebted to Dr. Lischer for this insightful quandary from his parish days, and also for his teaching role as professor of homiletics at Duke Divinity School, where he attempted to work his own miracle by teaching me to preach.

Chapter Three

2 Peck, M. Scott. *The Road Less Traveled.* New York: Simon & Schuster, 1978.

Chapter Four

3 Moyers, Bill. *Healing and the Mind,* 213–37. New York: Doubleday, 1993.

Chapter Six

4 *Newsweek,* November 10, 2003.

5 Moyers, Bill. *Healing and the Mind,* 343–63. New York: Doubleday, 1993.

6 Nouwen, Henri J. M. *The Wounded Healer.* New York: Doubleday, 1979.

7 Buechner, Frederick. *Wishful Thinking: A Theological ABC.* New York: Harper & Row, 1973.

Chapter Eight

8 Gulley, Philip. *Front Porch Tales,* 55–58. New York: HarperCollins, 1997.

9 Chang, Alicia. "Medical Miracles." Associated Press and *Indianapolis Star,* December 30, 2003, section E.

Rejoice in devotion

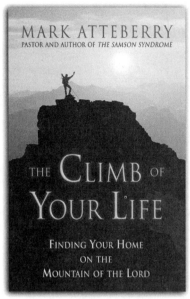

MARK ATTEBERRY
PASTOR AND AUTHOR OF *THE SAMSON SYNDROME*

THE CLIMB OF
YOUR LIFE

FINDING YOUR HOME
ON THE
MOUNTAIN OF THE LORD

Code #1991 • $12.95

Based on King David's famous mountain of the Lord passage in Psalm 24, this book offers you a new way of looking at your life of faith and, more importantly, a new and exciting way of living it.

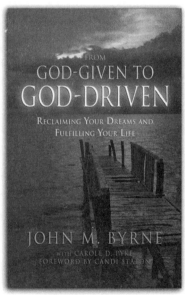

FROM
GOD-GIVEN TO
GOD-DRIVEN

RECLAIMING YOUR DREAMS AND
FULFILLING YOUR LIFE

JOHN M. BYRNE
with CAROLE D. PYKE
FOREWORD BY CANDI STATON

Code #1746 • $12.95

By learning from the teachings of this book, you will not only find happiness and purpose in your life, you will also become a beacon of faith to others.